DISCUSSION PAPER 76

I0122939

The African Union in Light of the Arab Revolts

An appraisal of the foreign policy and security objectives of South Africa, Ethiopia and Algeria

Edited by
MIKAEL ERIKSSON and LINNÉA GELOT

In cooperation with
The Swedish Defence Research Agency

NORDISKA AFRIKAINSTITUTET, UPPSALA 2013

Indexing terms:
African Union
Regional cooperation
Foreign policy
Foreign relations
International politics
Regional security
Algeria
Ethiopia
South Africa

Language checking: Peter Colenbrander

ISSN 1104-8417

ISBN 978-91-7106-735-7

© The author, editors, The Swedish Defence Research Agency and Nordiska Afrikainstitutet 2013

Production: Byrå4

Print on demand, Lightning Source UK Ltd.

Contents

Foreword

In 2012, the Swedish Defence Research Agency (FOI)[1] and the Nordic Africa Institute (NAI)[2] hosted a number of joint lectures on African security. The main objective of this collaboration during 2012 was to lay a solid basis for cooperation and capacity-building in Africa-related research on peace and security. In keeping with this objective, research cooperation on these issues has continued, as has the lecture series, which has become one of the key elements in this co-operation.

The theme of the 2012 lecture series was the political and institutional dynamics of the African Union (AU) in light of the Arab revolts. A particular puzzle was key member states political and security posture within the AU format. A sample of presentations are presented in this Discussion Paper series.[3]

Presentations on each state's role in the AU were made to a specialist audience of Swedish policy-makers and scholars working on peace, security and development in Africa. Presenters were carefully chosen from among a highly qualified group of experts interested in sharing their knowledge and experience with a Swedish audience. The convenors required that papers be of scientific standard and available for deposit. Each published lecture is intended to serve as a background reader for experts concerned with African peace and security.

The edited versions of the presentations each conveys a personal take on the theme of the joint lectures. The views, interpretations and any errors are those of the author, not of FOI or NAI, and authorship should be attributed to each presenter.

Mikael Eriksson and Linnéa Gelot
Co-Convenors
2012 Joint Lecture Series

---

1.   http://www.foi.se/en/Our-Knowledge/Security-policy-studies/Africa/Africa1/
2.   http://www.nai.uu.se/research/nai-foi%20lectures/
3.   See also paper by Okereke, C. Nna-Emeka, *Nigeria and the African Union in Light of the Arab Revolts.*

South Africa and the African Union

Thomas Kwasi Tieku

Introduction

Perhaps no single event has had profound impact on the African Union (AU) in the last ten years as the Arab revolt of 2010 and 2011. It led to the demise of two key AU supporters, the government of Hosni Mubarak in Egypt and the regime of Muammar Gaddafi in Libya. Both regimes strongly supported the 2006 reform of the AU funding formula that resulted in their countries, together with Algeria, Nigeria and South Africa, paying over 66 per cent of the annual contributions to the AU budget (Mkwezalamba 2006). The support for AU financial reform is one of many ways in which the two governments helped foster the growth of the AU in the last ten years.

The foundational ideas of the AU security architecture were agreed upon by African leaders during the Cairo summit hosted by Hosni Mubarak in Egypt in June 1993. The resulting 1993 Cairo Declaration on the Mechanism for Conflict Prevention, Management and Resolution and the annual AU High Level Retreat for Mediators and Special Envoys are the main reference points for any informed discussion of the AU security system. The 1999 Sirte summit, hosted by the regime of Ghaddafi, produced the AU, although journalistic accounts that attribute its formation to Ghaddafi's influence have been discredited in academic studies (Tieku 2004; Jeng 2012). The demise of Ghaddafi means that Africa has lost one of its strongest and most melodramatic campaigners for increased powers for the AU. Ghaddafi's death also marked the end (at least in the short term) of attempts by the continental union school of African politics to turn the AU into a continental African government.

The Arab revolt nearly destroyed relations between the AU, on one hand, and the UN and North Atlantic Treaty Organisation (NATO) on the other. But has the Arab revolt changed relations between the AU and South Africa? More precisely, has it opened the door for South Africa to dominate AU? On the surface, it seems the Arab revolt has done this. The fall of the Ghaddafi and of the Mubarak regimes and the pressure the revolt has put on the current Algerian government to pay more attention to domestic issues, coupled with Nigeria's internal insecurities, appear to give the remaining African powerhouse, the South African government, the opportunity to dictate to the AU. Fear of South African domination of the AU permeated the opposition to the candidacy of former South Africa Home Affairs Minister Nkosazana Dlamini-Zuma's for the chair of the AU Commission. Her election reinforced the dominant view that the African National Congress (ANC) government is preparing to coerce AU institutions into promoting the narrow foreign policy interests of South Africa (Allison 2012; Handy and Kjeldgaard 2012; Ojo 2012; *The Economist* 2012). These interests, articulated in the Medium-Term Strategic Framework (MTSF) to guide the Zuma government during the period 2009-14, are: promoting national interests or what the document calls closing the gap between domestic and foreign policy; promoting Southern African Development Community (SADC) integration; prioritisation of the African continent through 'African advancement'; strengthening South-South relations; improving strategic relations and strengthening political and economic relations with Northern states; and participating in the global system of governance (Government of the Republic of South Africa 2009; Landsberg 2012). This paper, however, draws on institutionalist argument (Pierson 2000; Tieku 2012b) to argue that AU norms, rules and organisational design make it almost impossible for any one state in Africa, including South Africa, to dictate the AU's direction and agenda. If anything, Dlamini-Zuma's leadership of the AU Commission makes it even harder for South Africa to influence the AU's course. The broad contours of AU priorities in the next few years have already been set.

The AU Commission is supposed to focus on administrative reforms, secure alternative funding for the AU and implement the plethora of decisions made by AU's political leaders. In addition, most observers expect the Dlamini-Zuma AU Commission to prioritise basic and prosaic necessities over the more dramatic firefighting issues, such as conflict resolution and management, which have enjoyed most of the AU's attention in the past ten years. The ANC government cannot direct the attention of AU away from these priority issues. As a shrewd political operative, Dlamini-Zuma is acutely aware that her successful bid for the chair of the AU Commission is largely due to her predecessor's failure to make meaningful progress in these four broad priority areas, and she is conscious of the stiff resistance she will encounter if she dares to refocus the Commission's attention elsewhere . Her stint at the helm of the pan-African organisation will be an unmitigated failure if the AU Commission makes few advances in these areas over the next four years.

The paper proceeds in four stages. The first explores the broader worldview that informs South Africa's approach to AU. The second section shows that discussions of South Africa-AU relations reflect conventional theoretical understanding of the behaviour of big states within international organisations. In the third part, South Africa-AU interactions over the past ten years are outlined, suggesting that South Africa has often been unable to prevail upon the AU to adopt its positions. Rather, the pan-African organisation has influenced South Africa to align its position with that of the AU on several major issues. The section also outlines the direction the AU is likely to take over the next four years with Dlamini-Zuma as Commission chair, given that this course has already been decided and she can do little about it. The conclusion sketches the 'institutional logic' that shows why it is almost impossible for South Africa or any other big African state to dictate the AU's course.

Master Frame of South Africa-AU Relations

The current South African government looks at the AU through a particular ideological lens. Understanding this broader ideological framework is the key to gaining a good insight into South Africa-AU relations.

The Zuma government approaches the AU through the lens of a classic African statist school (Mashabane 2009). The Africa statists see the AU, and indeed any international organisation of which their states are members, as a purely intergovernmental enterprise (Maloka 2001; Matthews 2001). Because they dislike international organisations that have a supranational identity, they often resist efforts to entrust international organisation with meaningful responsibilities without close supervision by agencies within their states (Padelford 1964; Maloka 2001). For them, international organisation exists primarily to promote the foreign policy interests of their governments (Padelford 1964; Maloka 2001). The African statists loathe any attempt to endow the AU with supranational powers. As President Zuma's foreign minister, Maite Nkoana-Mashabane (2009), succinctly put it in relation to the decision to transform the AU Commission into the AU Authority, 'the decision … will have to be implemented within the context of our understanding of the African Union as an intergovernmental organisation of sovereign member states.' African statists take this position because they consider the colonial division of Africa into states as a useful organising principle (Woronoff 1970). Many who hold this view are openly critical of colonial rule, and they also refer to the boundaries created by colonial authorities as fraudulent and artificial (Wallerstein 1967). Even so, they feel the demarcations are worth preserving. For this paradigmatic group, the maintenance and protection of the state system in Africa ought to be the guiding principle of interstate cooperation (Woronoff 1970). They think interstate cooperation in Africa should take the form of loose relationships of economic interdependency along the lines of the European Union, and/or mere coordination of common interests (Nyerere 1963; Nye 1966).

As with every paradigmatic group or worldview, there are subtle differences within the statist school. Some proponents of statist ideas are absolute statists, loathing attempts to cede any aspect of sovereignty, however insignificant, to a supranational authority. The absolute statist group was led by Liberia's William Tubman and Madagascar's Philibert Tsiranana during the first pan-African debate of the 1960s (Woronoff 1970). African leaders such as Uganda's Yoweri

Museveni became the major advocates of this position during the grand debate in Accra in 2006 (Murithi 2008). Other members of the statist school are willing, though not without protest, to cede some authority to major international organisations in Africa if such powers do not undermine the core sovereign prerogatives of their states. The latter group, which I label the statist-interdependency group, is usually willing to cede sovereign prerogatives in the economic realm to a supranational organisation. Nigeria's Tafawa Balewa, Tanzania's Julius Nyerere and Côte d'Ivoire's Félix Houphouët-Boigny were the leading advocates of the statist-interdependency group in the 1960s pan-African debate (Nyerere 1963). The governments of South Africa and Botswana were leading promoters of the statist-interdependency ideas during the 2006 grand debate (Murithi 2008).

The statist position is fiercely opposed by the continental unionists, whose stand is influenced by the ideas of Pan-Africanism and, in particular, Marcus Garvey's 'Back to Africa' movement. Continental unionists hold that the inhabitants of the African region should be organised within a continent-wide political matrix (Nkrumah 1963; Nye 1966; Maloka 2001; Tieku 2006). For those who hold this view, a continent-wide union with 'a unified economic planning, a unified military and defence strategy, and a unified foreign policy and diplomacy,' is the more appropriate political system (Nkrumah 1963). Continent-wide union in the form of federation, confederation or something similar would be more apposite, because it would provide the tools for African people to resist foreign domination and oppression and promote unity and economic independence, and it is also the most effective way to develop a common African culture (Nkrumah 1963; Maloka 2001).

Given such premises, the school inevitably regards the African state system as illegitimate and problematic. Proponents of this view see the system as illegitimate in part because they believe the people who inhabit Africa were prohibited from making a contribution to the establishment of the boundaries that created the state system, and in part because they think the present system reversed the organic development of political organisations and institutions (Nkrumah 1963). They also see it as problematic because of the many challenges created by the arbitrary division of African societies into states. African elites that subscribe to the continent-wide political framework therefore called for the rebuilding of African political communities. They want a new form of community with an African flavour to replace the state system they inherited from European colonial rule.

Will the Zuma government push the AU to promote the statist-interdependency agenda, giving that Gaddafi, the main defender of continental unionist ideas over the last 20 years, is gone and a former South African Home Affairs Minister is comfortably seated on the chair of the AU Commission? Conventional narratives provide an affirmative answer (Handy and Kjeldgaard 2012; Ojo 2012). They expect African powerhouses such as South Africa, Nigeria,

Egypt, Algeria and Libya to determine the AU's priorities. Except for Libya, these are the economically and militarily powerful states of Africa. The five together pay 66 per cent of the annual assessed contributions to the regular budget of the AU. In 2012, for instance, they will collectively pay US$81.2 million of the US$123 million of assessed contributions (African Union 2012:5). The other 49 members will pay a meagre 34 per cent of the budget. Based on this observation, it may appear logical to think these five states will pull all the strings at the AU, including determining the key issues and the agenda the AU pursues.

Conventional Narratives of South Africa-AU Relations

In the view of conventional thinkers on African politics, it makes sense to see South Africa – the largest, most industrialised economy in Africa, the only African member of the G20 and a self-described genuine emerging power in Africa – to be the main driver of the AU. This view was used in opposing the candidacy of Dlamini-Zuma. Paul-Simon Handy and Stine Kjeldgaard (2012) from the Institute for Security Studies, the highly respected South African thinktank, claim that South Africa wants to use Dlamini-Zuma 'to control the AU Commission to boost its bid for a permanent seat at the UN Security Council,' to 'stamp its hegemony on the continent' and to affirm 'its record as the only African country to belong to the G20 and BRICS.' In the opinion of the Kenya-based political analyst Alexander Ojo (2012), Dlamini-Zuma's quest to chair the AU Commission reflects 'the unbridled ambition of South Africa and the capacity it has to "foist its Interior Minister Dr. Nkosazana Dlamini-Zuma on the (African) continent".' For these thinkers, there is little doubt that Dlamini-Zuma 'would be taking her orders from Pretoria' (Handy and Kjeldgaard 2012).

Though none of the conventional narrators used the word 'realism,' their arguments are rooted in a realist paradigm of international organisations. Scholars of this genre, especially the intergovernmentalists, think that international organisations (IOs) such as AU are mere tools of powerful states (Grieco 1996, 1997, 1999; Owen 2002; Pedersen 1998). One strand of realist school claims that IOs reflect preference convergence of global or regional powers (Keohane and Hoffmann 1991; Moravcsik 1997). Scholars using preference convergence theory argue that big states in IOs bargain among themselves to reach common denominator interests and form international organisations to increase their power vis-à-vis new global forces. Small states within the region join the organisation because they think the institutional mechanisms will help them manage their interconnectedness with the big states. Joseph Grieco (1995:34) calls this the 'voice opportunities thesis.' The behaviour and direction of these organisations depend heavily on politics and bargaining between the big states.

From this realist perspective, it appears the largest countries in Africa have the potential to drive the AU agenda and direction, in much the same way as, according to realist-inspired works, the biggest European states – Germany, France and Britain – dominate the European Union. It is perhaps unsurprising that some observers see South Africa as the main driver of the AU. The selection of Dlamini-Zuma as AU Commission chair has emboldened realist-inspired conjecture that the ANC government will redirect the AU to focus on narrow South African foreign policy interests.

South Africa's Influence and AU Politics

Talk of South Africa dominance of the AU is grounded in misconception and poor understanding of AU institutional structures and of the ideational foundation of continental African politics. It ignores the fact that the chairperson of the AU, and indeed AU bureaucrats, are forbidden by AU rules from serving the narrow interests of any member state. According to article 4(1) of the Statute of the Commission of African Union 'members of the Commission and the other staff shall not seek or receive instructions from any government or from any other authority external to the Union' (African Union 2002). Her moves will be watched closely, but she is savvy enough to know the inherent danger and cost of her appearing as a 'puppet doll' of South Africa.

At the institutional level, and in practice, the office of chairperson of the AU does not have the powers assumed by those who think South Africa will use it to dominate the AU. Though the chairperson is the chief executive officer and ultimate accounting officer of the AU Commission, in practice previous chairpersons have acted like ceremonial heads of state. The eight AU commissioners and the Commission's deputy chairperson have often acted as independent players. As the panel of AU auditors pointed out in its findings:

> The Panel finds no basis for both the perception and practice that the Deputy Chairperson has sole responsibility for the administration and finances of the Commission. In the performance of his/her duties, the Deputy Chairperson is ultimately answerable to the Chairperson who is the Accounting Officer of the Commission. Similarly, the Panel finds no basis that the Commissioners, by virtue of their election by the Assembly, have no direct accountability to the Chairperson in his capacity as the Chief Executive Officer (AU Audit Report 2007: 44).

The eight commissioners often do not report to the chairperson because they are independently elected by the Assembly of Heads of State and Government of the AU and the Commission chair has no power to hire, sack or even discipline any of them. The Bureau of the Deputy Commissioner has become somewhat independent of the office of the chairperson, in part because of the selection processes but also because almost all the administrative units report to this bureau rather than to the office of the chairperson. Only the Directorate of Women,

Gender and Development, the Citizens Directorate, as well as AU Representational and Specialised Office report to the bureau of the chair of AU Commission. The independence of the eight commissioners and the dependence of the chair of the commission on the deputy chair for the management of the AU budget and staff make the chairperson's bureau institutionally weak. Past chairpersons, including the authoritative Alpha Konaré, who assumed the chair with the aura of a former president and history professor, could not overcome these structural limitations on his office. It is unlikely the more reserved Madam Zuma will be able to change the power dynamics overnight or at all, especially given that her deputy and the more powerful commissioners, such as the Commissioner for Peace and Security, are backed by other major African states and have more experience working for the Commission.

At the individual level, as a former foreign minister Madam Dlamini-Zuma is acutely aware that the AU is not the best institution to promote the narrow foreign policy goals articulated in the MTSF. For one thing, the AU is not well equipped to help South Africa close the gap between domestic and foreign policies. This job can be executed much better by the South African Ministry of International Relations and Cooperation and the ANC party. One cannot imagine President Zuma's government getting the AU involved in a purely domestic consultative and policy development process. Neither has the AU the capacity to assist South Africa in building strong bilateral relations with traditional and emerging powers. Nor is the AU in a good position to serve as a vehicle for South Africa to pursue its strategic interests in global governance institutions. The chairperson is politically astute enough to know that the future of the AU, and the renewal of her mandate, will depend heavily on how well she delivers on four key priority issues.

First, Dlamini-Zuma is leading the AU Commission at a time when it needs fundamental institutional renewal and administrative reform. There will be tremendous pressure on her to implement the recommendation of the 2007 AU Audit Report and to halt the rapid growth of administrative inefficiencies in the last few years. She is also expected to put the Commission in a position to play the leadership role envisioned by the founders of the AU (Audit of African Union 2007).

Second, she will be under enormous pressure to implement the high-level panel report on alternative sources of financing, which recommended a number of options, including a US$2 hospitality levy per stay in a hotel; a five cents (US) levy per text message sent; and a US$5 travel levy on flights to and from Africa (Cilliers and Okeke 2012:4).

Third, the AU's political leaders signalled during the January 2012 summit that they expect the Commission to implement within four years the plethora of decisions they have made in the last ten years. Among them is a 2007 decision to turn the AU Commission into the AU Authority, a move supposed to enhance the powers and supranationality of the Commission. As the then AU Commission Chairperson Jean Ping indicated, '[we] are creating an institution with a bigger mandate, with bigger capacities, which moves us toward the goal of the union government' (*AU Monitor* 2007). Though the exact powers of the Authority have yet to be determined, Ping claimed that '[t]he body will be headed by a president and a vice-president, and the commissioners will become secretaries' (*AU Monitor* 2007). Dlamini-Zuma will be under intense pressure to implement this transformation. Many observers will be watching this closely because South Africa is among minority of countries opposed to turning the AU Commission into a supranational institution. As the South Africa Minister for International Relations and Cooperation, Maite Nkoana-Mashabane (2009) argued:

> The decision on the African Union Authority will have to be implemented within the context of our understanding of the African Union as an intergovernmental organisation of sovereign member states. It is not our understanding that the African Union Authority will be a supranational entity operating over our heads.

Finally, the Dlamini-Zuma AU Commission is expected to turn the AU's attention to basic needs such as food security, governance, gender mainstreaming, inter-state infrastructure development and conflict prevention. The four AU priorities are big ticket items that require urgent attention over the next four years. Dlamini-Zuma will commit political suicide in pan-African and even South African politics (because her chances of becoming South Africa president or leader of another major international organisation will diminish if she is perceived as a failure at a continental level) if she turns her attention from them to focus on narrow South African concerns.

More fundamentally, the AU is institutionally designed to make it difficult for a single member to determine its agenda and policies. The best route any member has to influence the organisation is through the intergovernmental political organs of the AU, namely the Assembly, the Executive Council and the Permanent Representative Council.[4] They are supposed to create and direct policy initiatives, but in practice have been unable to carry out these responsibilities and have become heavily dependent on the AU Commission for fresh ideas, policy direction and innovative policies (for a detailed explanation of why this is the case, see Tieku 2012b). The AU Commission is, however, structured such that one or few AU members cannot determine its priorities, agenda and future directions. First, the technocratic and eclectic workings of the Commission leave little room for member states to drive its agenda. For instance, the Commission uses informal channels and mechanisms to generate most agenda

---

4.　This section draws on Tieku (2012b).

items for AU summits, though the AU rule is that such items can come from any AU organ, member states and regional economic communities. In fact, most items for summit meetings are developed during sectoral expert meetings, which are informal institutional mechanisms with 'no formal basis in the AU legal framework' (Kane and Mbelle 2007:12). It is impossible for a single state or a few to dominate these sectoral expert meetings. This is why less than 30 per cent of agenda items for AU summits in the last ten years have come from African states, including South Africa (interview with former Ghanaian ambassador to the AU, 16 February 2012). Specifically, the South Africa mission in Addis Ababa and the African section of South Africa's foreign affairs ministry are ill-equipped to play a leading role in sectoral meetings.

In any case, AU Commission rules prohibit those who organise sectoral meetings from soliciting direction or advice from AU member states. Dismissal is often the punishment for those who breach this rule. At the same time, AU member states are prohibited from influencing AU Commission staff. As stipulated in article 4(2) of the Statute of the Commission of the African Union 'each Member State undertakes to respect the exclusive character of the responsibilities of the Members of the Commission and the other staff and shall not influence or seek to influence them in the discharge of their responsibilities.' In other words, the ANC government will be breaking a cardinal AU rule if South African government officials try to use the office of the chair of AU Commission or any staffer to pursue South Africa's narrow foreign policy interests.

At the ideational level, the founders of the AU drew lessons from the anti-colonial and anti-hegemonic ideology of the pan-African national character when they designed AU institutions so as not to become dependent on a single or even a few member states. The solidaristic social structure in which the AU is embedded often restricts member states from playing hard power politics. Most decisions by AU institutions are based on consensus rather than competitive voting. Even when AU members do vote, the votes usually affirm agreements already reached informally. Because consensus decision-making often confers *de facto* veto powers on even the most powerless members of a group, powerful African states are forced to treat each AU member as an equal. The deference to compromise outcomes means no single African state can impose its preferences on the rest, or force weaker members to accept agreements they oppose.

Moreover, the South Africa domination thesis neglects the reality that the South Africa government lacks the resources and material power to provide the incentives that regional hegemons in the European Union project, such as Germany, France and Britain, are able to give their smaller European counterparts. South Africa cannot offer sufficient incentives or side payments, or make plausible enough threats, to induce other African governments to behave in a particular way. It has neither the ideational clout in Addis Ababa to frame issues in such a way that they appeal to larger constituencies, nor the economic resources to make side payments and provide continental public goods. Indeed, it lacks the required ideational and economic power to set, maintain and enforce AU rules. Its 13 per cent contribution to the AU budget – around US$16 million of US$123 million in 2012 – is not substantial enough to allow the Zuma government to use it as a major bargaining chip. The AU will not be inordinately inconvenienced if South Africa does not pay its regular budget share. Domestic problems – an estimated unemployment rate of more than 25 per cent, widespread poverty in core ANC constituencies, welfare payments to more than 13.8 million, growing social dissatisfaction, xenophobic attacks on other Africans and a limited tax base – coupled with the current South African government's limited ability to develop independent and broad-based ideas attractive to other African governments limit South Africa's regional hegemonic ambitious.

South Africa's foreign policy concerns under Zuma (outlined above) are so remote from the issues the AU needs to focus on in the next decade that it will take a momentous shift to align the two. However, the historical record of South Africa-AU relations suggests the former lacks the capacity to change the policies and decisions made by the latter. The way in which South Africa and AU handled the post-election conflicts in Côte D'Ivoire and the Libyan crisis illustrate South Africa's inability to change decisions made by AU organs. In the Côte d'Ivoire crisis, South Africa took a pro- Gbagbo position, while AU took pro-Ouattara decisions throughout the crisis. The AU and ECOWAS (Economic Community of West African States) were the first institutions to recognise Ouattara as the winner of the 28 November 2010 elections. In a press statement released after its 251st meeting in Addis Ababa on 4 December 2010, the AU Peace and Security Council sided with the provisional results released by Côte d'Ivoire's independent electoral commission (IEC) on 3 December 2010, which showed that Ouattara had won. In reference to Côte d'Ivoire's constitutional court's annulment of the IEC results, the Peace and Security Council 'expressed AU's total rejection of any attempt to create a *fait accompli* to undermine the electoral process and the will of the people as expressed on 28 November 2010' (AU 2010a). At its 252nd meeting, held on 9 December 2010, the Peace and Security Council formally recognised Ouattara as 'the President Elect of Côte d'Ivoire,' and called on Gbagbo 'to respect the results of the election and to facilitate, without delay, the transfer of power to the President Elect' (African Union 2010b). It suspended Côte d'Ivoire from participating in the activities of the AU until Gbagbo left office. The chairperson of the AU Commission, Jean Ping, initially asked former South African President Thabo Mbeki to lead the AU's diplomatic effort to force Gbagbo to resign, but he was replaced by the Kenyan Prime Minister Raila Odinga when it became obvious that South Africa actually wanted Gbagbo to stay in power (AfricanNews 2010).

Unlike the AU, South Africa initially stood by Laurent Gbagbo, and was even accused of providing military support to the beleaguered Ivorian leader. As the then president of ECOWAS Commission James Victor Gbeho put it, '[as] we talk now there is a South African warship docked in Cote d'Ivoire. Now actions such as that can only complicate the matter further' (Reuters New 2011; New24 2011). After failing to make the Peace and Security Council and AU Commission take pro-Gbagbo positions, South Africa tried unsuccessfully to get the support of African leaders at the January AU summit for rescinding the Peace and Security Council and Commission decisions recognising Ouattara as the winner of the elections (*Zimbabwe Mail* 2011). James Victor Gbeho seems to have captured the consensual view of a majority of African leaders when he said:

> The disappointment was that in spite of the solidarity of the AU and the international community, certain member States of AU (i.e. South Africa and Angola) came to the meeting (i.e. January 2011 AU Summit) and reopened the whole issue, judging that the AU and the ECOWAS made a mistake in accepting Ouattara as President (Panapress 2011).

The ANC government was roundly criticised for second-guessing the decision of AU organs and changed its position to align it with the AU's shortly after the summit.

Similarly, while the AU opposed military intervention in Libya from beginning to end, South Africa voted in favour of UN Resolution 1973 authorising military intervention in the North African country. The Zuma government changed its position and became a vocal critic of the Libya bombings only after widespread condemnation of its position by the AU leadership and after South African trade unions and the ANC youth wing joined other Africans on 23 March 2011 to protest the NATO bombings (Malema 2011). The divergent positions of South Africa and the AU became a major political crisis and are a good indication of the overall influence of South Africa in the AU system. It would have been impossible for the AU to take a stand on these major political crises different from the Zuma government's if South Africa had been a classic hegemonic player within the AU system.

Furthermore, it is generally agreed that South Africa under President Zuma lacks the moral, intellectual, political and rhetorical capital needed to command a large following among other African states (Vines 2010). Part of the problem is that President Zuma is widely seen in African political circles as an intellectual and political lightweight. On a continent where titles and degrees count so much, perceptions of the leader of a big state as both intellectually and politically weak makes it difficult for even the smallest of states to follow that large state. President Zuma compounded this problem by allowing his government to take a more reticent approach towards engagement with other African states

(Vines 2010). He has replaced the pan-African rhetoric and idealism associated with the Mandela and Mbeki governments with populist rhetoric that places more emphasis on South Africa's domestic material concerns and on conveying a message that South Africa is interested in creating jobs for South Africans and in reducing poverty domestically, especially in ANC strongholds. Thus, the rhetoric of the Zuma government is a clear departure from that of previous post-apartheid governments, which often created the impression that South Africa's economic diplomacy was aimed at transforming the economies of the entire continent. The statist orientation of the Zuma government has not been well received in other African states (Vines 2010; Landsberg 2012). This disappointment is particularly apparent in countries such as Nigeria and Ghana that supported and hosted the ANC leadership during the liberation struggle. It is common to hear political elites in these countries complain that the Zuma government lacks the foresight to maintain and build upon the special efforts Mandela and Mbeki made to integrate post-apartheid South Africa into the African international system.

Unlike the Mandela and Mbeki administrations, the Zuma government has concentrated on showcasing South Africa as the undisputed regional hegemon in Africa. This public display of power and departure from Mandela and Mbeki's sensitivity to the unfavourable perception of South Africa as hegemon is loathed in relatively powerful states such as Algeria, Ethiopia, Kenya and Nigeria, which had good relations with South Africa under Mandela and Mbeki. The moves by the Zuma government appear to be a strategic mistake, as they challenge the pan-African national character, which rejects power as a basis for international relations. As William Zartman has pointed out, not only the African ruling class 'rejects relations on the basis of power', rejection of 'power as a basis for international relations' is also a national characteristic of almost all African states (Zartman 1967). Besides the challenge that Zuma's hegemony-seeking behaviour poses to the ideational foundation of the AU, the Zuma administration seems to forget that resentment towards powerful states runs deep in the thinking of Africa's elites. That resentment often compels African ruling elites to mobilise against any hegemony seeker and makes it hard for relatively big and wealthy African states to garner support for their positions. It is, perhaps, unsurprising that Ethiopia, Kenya and Nigeria became the public face of the group of states that opposed the candidacy of Dlamini-Zuma, even though it was widely known among the leaders of these states that she is qualified for the job. The only reason her candidacy became controversial was because of South Africa. Her election might have been a cakewalk if she had come from a smaller African state. Thus, it is often difficult for the big states, and South Africa in particular, to get their way.

Conclusion

This paper has tried to show that although the Arab revolt has changed AU relations in many ways, they have not altered AU–South Africa relations. The collapse of major Arab regimes as a result of the revolts and the pressure these put on other Arab governments to address domestic economic and political concerns has not in any way given the South African government licence to dominate the AU. The pan-African national character, which loathes power-based international relations, discourages hegemonic and power-seeking behaviour by African states, including South Africa. The ANC government will face stiff resistance if it dares to play the part of classic regional hegemon. The pan-African national character will encourage other African government to oppose every hegemonic move by South Africa in the AU system.

The consensus political game played in the AU system, where every member is a potential veto holder, is not conducive to the realpolitik some analysts think South African government will play in the AU in coming years. It is even unclear whether the current South African government has the leadership and intellectual qualities or the political will and appetite to play a regional hegemonic role in Africa. Major internal problems and the South African government's limited capacity to generate ideas and disseminate them in Africa may pose a major challenge to South Africa's hegemonic aspirations. Political missteps, including the controversial support for Laurent Gbagbo and for UN resolution 1973, and the state-centric rhetoric associated with the Zuma government have tarnished the South Africa brand and the country's pan-African credentials. More fundamentally, administrative rules, institutional norms and decision-making procedures of AU Commission make it difficult for a single African state or a small collection of African states to drive and dictate AU policies, agendas and directions. The AU Commission relies on expertise and technocratic skills that South Africa alone cannot supply nor does South African have a collection of experts at its embassy in Addis Ababa that can dictate to their counterparts in other African states.

An important policy message from the above discussion is that AU is not an institution easily manipulated by even its materially dominant members. Material capabilities do not necessarily translate into influence in the AU system. In some cases, material endowments can be a liability in that they often make other AU members suspicious of moves by so-called African powerhouses. Material resources are often not assets in continental African politics because the pan-African national character usually encourages smaller and medium-sized African states to gang up against positions taken by big African states. Indeed, materially weak but ideationally resourceful AU members often have more influence within the AU than their big counterparts. Small AU members with smart diplomats in Addis Ababa and sharp experts at AU meetings have a greater chance of influencing the direction of the AU than materially power-ful members whose missions in Addis are staffed by average people and whose experts attending AU meetings are second-rate. Another policy lesson to draw from the paper is that it may be easier to influence the AU through the Commis-sion, in particular through the eight AU departments and the two units, than by trying to work through the political organs. The Commission is the brain of the AU and whoever controls the head could also direct the body. It would, however, be mistaken to think the office of AU Commission chairperson is the cortex of the AU brain. The eight commissioners are the cortex in their own way and building and developing strategic relationships with them may offer more leverage and influence than working through the chairperson or the govern-ments of big AU member states.

References

African Union (2002). 'Statute of the Commission of African Union.' African Union, Durban: South Africa. Available at: http://www.au2002.gov.za/docs/summit_council/statutes.pdf

– (2007). 'Audit Report of the African Union.' Available at: http://www.pambazuka.org/actionalerts/images/uploads/AUDIT_REPORT.doc

– (2010a). 'Press Statement of the 251st Meeting of the Peace and Security Council.' Available at: http://www.ausitroom-psd.org/Documents/PSC2010/251st/PressstatementCI.pdf

– (2010b). 'Communiqué of the 252nd Meeting of the Peace and Security Council.' Addis Ababa. available at: http://www.africa-union.org/root/au/Conferences/2010/december/Communiqu%C3%A9%20of%20the%20252nd.pdf

– (2012). 'The Financial Year for the African Union, 2012 Doc.EX.CL/721 (XXI), African Union, Addis Ababa.

AU Monitor (2007). 'AU to be Transformed into Union Authority.' Available at: http://www.pambazuka.org/aumonitor/comments/2145/

Allison, Simon (2012). 'Dear Nkosazana: Beware of great expectations.' Available at: http://dailymaverick.co.za/article/2012-10-15-dear-nkosazana-beware-of-great-expectations.

Cilliers Jakkie, and Jide Martyns Okeke (2012). 'The Election of Dr. Dlamini-Zuma as AU Chairperson: Towards Pan-Africanism and African Renaissance.' Available at: www.wacsi.org/attachment/131.

COMESA-EAC-SADC Tripartite Summit Communique (2011). Summit was held at Johannesburg in the Republic of South Africa. Available at: http://www.sadc.int/english/current-affairs/news/communique-of-the-second-comesa-eac-sadc-tripartite-summit/

Evans, Graham (1999). 'South Africa's Foreign Policy after Mandela: Mbeki and his Concept of an African Renaissance.' *The Round Table* 352, no. 1: 622

Government of the Republic of South Africa (2009a). 'Medium-Term Strategic Framework (MTSF), Guide to Government's Programme for the Electoral Mandate Period 2009–2014.' August. Pretoria-Tshwane: Treasury.

– (2009b). 'President Zuma concludes inaugural State visit to Angola.' Available online at: http://www.thepresidency.gov.za/pebble.asp?relid=961.

Grieco, M. Joseph (1995). 'The Maastricht Treaty, Economic and Monetary Union, and the Neo-Realist Research Program,' *Review of International Studies* 21, no. 1:21–40.

– (1996). 'State Interests and International Rule Trajectories: A Neorealist Interpretation of the Maastricht Treaty and European Economic and Monetary Union.' *Security Studies* 5, no. 2:261–305.

– (1997). 'Systemic Sources of Variation in Regional Institutionalisation in Western Europe, East Asia, and the Americas.' In *The Political Economy of Regionalism* edited by Edward D. Mansfield and Helen V. Milner. Pages 164–87. New York: Columbia University Press.

– (1999). 'Realism and Regionalism: American Power and German and Japanese Institutional Strategies During and After the Cold War.' In *Unipolar Politics*, edited by Ethan B. Kapstein and Michael Mastanduno. Pages 319–53. New York: Columbia University Press.

Handy, S. Paul, and Stine Kjeldgaard (2012). 'Analysis: SA bid for AU chair a dicey one.' Available at: www.thenewage.co.za/blogdetail.aspx?mid=186&blog_id=%20 1688

Jeng, Abou (2012). *Peacebuilding in the African Union: Law, Philosophy, and Practice.* Cambridge: Cambridge University Press.

Keohane O. Robert, and Stanley Hoffmann (eds.) (1991). *The New European Community: Decision-Making and Institutional Change.* Boulder: Westview Press.

– (2000). 'Globalisation: What's New? What's Not? (And So What?).' Foreign Policy 118:104–19.

Landsberg, Chris (2012). 'The Jacob Zuma Government's Foreign Policy: Association or Dissociation?' *Austral: Brazilian Journal of Strategy and International Relations* 1, no. 1:76.

Malema, Julius (7 July 2011). 'SA unions and ANCYL protest against NATO bombings.' Available at: http://www.youtube.com/watch?v=8gMA5zRJUa8.

Maloka, Eddy (ed.) (2001), *A United States of Africa.* Pretoria: African Institute of South Africa.

Mandela, Nelson (1993). 'South Africa's Future Foreign Policy,' *Foreign Affairs* 72, no. 5. Available at: www.foreignaffairs.org/19931201faessay5221/nelson-mandela/ south-africa-s-future-foreign-policy.html

– (30 July 1998). 'Maiden Speech to Assembly of OAU Heads of State and Government.' Available at: http://www.anc.org.za/ancdocs/history/mandela/1998/ sp980608.html

– (1999). 'Speech to Assembly of OAU Heads of State and Government at the 30th ordinary session of Organisation of African Unity.' Tunis. Available at: http://www. anc.org.za/ancdocs/history/mandela/1998/sp980608.html

Maxwell Mkwezalamba (29 May, 2006). Statement on the Occasion of the Opening of the Meeting of Governmental Experts on Alternative Sources of Financing the African Union (African Union, Addis Ababa). Available at http://www.africa-union. org/root/UA/Conferences/Mai/EA/29mai/WELCOME%20STATEMENT%20 %20Alternative%20source%20of%20funding.pdf

Murithi, Tim (ed.) (2008). *Towards a Union Government for Africa: Challenges and Opportunities*. Institute for Security Studies. Cape Town.

Nkoana-Mashabane, Maite (2009). 'Speech delivered by Minister for International Relations and Cooperation. Maite Nkoana-Mashabane during the Ministerial Outreach programme at the University of Limpopo, 16 October.' Available at: http://www.info.gov.za/speech/DynamicAction?pageid=461&sid=4843&tid=4988

Nkrumah, Kwame (1963). *African Must Unite*. London: Heinemann.

Nye, Joseph S. (1966). *Pan-Africanism and East African Integration*. Cambridge MA: Harvard University Press.

Nyerere, Julius (1963). 'A United States of Africa,' *Journal of Modern African Studies* 1, no. 1, pp. 1–6.

Ojo, Alexander (9 July 2012). 'Facts, Fallacies of Race for African Union Commission Chairperson.' *People's Daily*. Available at: www.peoplesdaily-online.com/index. php/news/news/foreign-news/1682-facts-and-fallacies-of-race-for-african-union-commission-chairperson-ii

Olivier, Gerrit, and Deon Geldenhuys (1997). 'South Africa's Foreign Policy: From Idealism to Pragmatism.' *Business and the Contemporary World* 9, no. 2:365–6

Owen, M. John (2001). 'Transnational Liberalism and U.S. Primacy.' *International Security* 26:117–52.

Padelford, Norman J. (1964). 'The Organisation of African Unity,' *International Organisation* 18, no. 3:521–42.

Panapress (2011). 'South Africa Slams NATO Bombing of Libya in United Nations Speech.' Available at: http://panafricannews.blogspot.ca/2011/06/south-africa-slams-nato-bombing-of.html

Pedersen, Thomas (1998). *Germany, France and the Integration of Europe: A Realist Interpretation*. London: Pinter.

Pierson, Paul (2000). Increasing Returns, Path Dependence, and the Study of Politics. *American Political Science Review* 94, no. 2:251-67.

Reuters and News24 (8 February, 2011). 'Ecowas Miffed at SA Navy Ship to Ivory Coast,' available at: http://www.news24.com/SouthAfrica/News/Ecowas-miffed-at-SA-warship-in-Ivory-Coast-20110208

RFI (2010). 'AU chair calls for Gbagbo to step down.' Available at : http://www. english.rfi.fr/africa/20101208-au-chair-calls-gbagbo-step-down or http://www. news24.com/Africa/News/AU-calls-on-Gbagbo-to-step-down

Schraeder, J. Peter (2001). 'South Africa's Foreign Policy from International Pariah to leader of the African Renaissance.' *The Round Table* 359, no. 1:229–43.

The Economist (21 July 2012). 'The top spot in Africa's most powerful club goes to a South African,' Available at http://www.economist.com/node/21559397

Tieku, Kwasi Thomas (2004). Explaining the clash and accommodation of interests of major actors in the creation of the African Union. *African Affairs* 103, 249–67.

– (2012a). 'A Pan-African View of A "New" Agenda for Peace,' *International Journal* 67. no. 2. 373–389.

– (2012b). 'The evolution and role of AU Commission and Africrats: Drivers of Africa's regionalism.' In *The Research Companion to Regionalisms*, edited by Andrew Grant, Scarlett Cornelissen and Tim Shaw. Farham: Ashgate.

Vines, Alex (2010). 'South Africa's politics of peace and security in Africa.' *South African Journal of International Affairs* 17, no. 1:53–63.

Wallerstein, Immanuel (1967). *Africa: The Politics of Unity*. New York: Random House.

Woronoff, Jon (1970). *Organizing African Unity*. Metuchen: Scarecrow Press.

Zartman, William (1967). 'Africa as a Subordinate State System in International Relations.' *International Organization* 21, no. 4:545–64.

Zimbabwe Mail (8 February 2011). 'South Africa joins Zimbabwe in supplying arms to Gbagbo,' Available at: http://www.thezimbabwemail.com/world/7279.html

Ethiopia and the African Union

Mehari Taddele Maru

Introduction

This article investigates Ethiopia's contributions to and its influence on the African Union (AU). It also explains and analyses the role its leaders played in the Organisation of African Unity (OAU) and in the AU. Since most of the important initiatives by Ethiopia on the peace and security of the Horn of Africa have been advanced and implemented through Intergovernmental Authority on Development (IGAD) and passed to the AU, indirectly Ethiopia's influence on the AU also reflects its role in IGAD.

Ethiopia has made major contributions to the OAU/AU in five areas. First, Ethiopia's historical background served as the seedbed from which the pan-African solidarity movement drew inspiration, culminating in the creation of the OAU in 1963. Second, Ethiopia extended enormous political support to various anti-colonial and anti-apartheid struggles in Africa, including military training, material and diplomatic support to liberation movements in South Africa, Zimbabwe and Namibia.[1] As the first independent black African nation to be a member of the League of Nations and also as a founding member of the UN, Ethiopia promoted and defended the interests of Africa in various global forums. Together with Liberia, Ethiopia indicted the South African apartheid government at the International Court of Justice. Third, since the Korean War in the 1950s and the Congo crisis in 1960s, Ethiopia has been one of the top African troop-contributing countries to UN and AU peacekeeping missions. The recent peacekeeping mission to the disputed area of Abyei is entirely composed of Ethiopian troops, and is unique in the history of peacekeeping for various reasons.[2] Ethiopia has also made significant contributions to mediation efforts, particularly in crises in its neighbourhood, particularly Somalia and Sudan.

Fourth, as the host country for the AU headquarters and the seat of various multilaterally and bilaterally accredited missions, delegations and institutions, Addis Ababa is the diplomatic hub of Africa. This, in the words of Ethiopia's current foreign policy strategy document, requires the country to "carry a spe-

---

1. South-West Africa Cases (Ethiopia v. South Africa; Liberia v. South Africa); Second Phase Address, available from http://www.unhcr.org/refworld/docid/4023a9414.html (accessed 12 November 2012); Nelson Mandela (1995), *Long Walk to Freedom: The Autobiography of Nelson Mandela*. London: Little Brown & Co.; Emperor Haile Sellasie, *Africa's Independence Day,* speech, April 1963.

2. Mehari Taddele Maru, (2012), *"The Contributions of Ethiopia to the Abyei Peacekeeping Force"*, Institute for Security Studies, ISS Today, available http://www.iss.co.za/iss_today.php?ID=1358 (accessed 31 March 2013).

cial responsibility for the organization [the AU]."[3] The close to 500 embassies, diplomatic missions and international organisations from all over the world accredited to the AU and Ethiopia make Addis Ababa one of the five biggest diplomatic concentrations in the world.

Fifth, based on capacity to pay and GDP, Ethiopia regularly pays its assessed contribution of US$ 1.4 million per year to the AU. While 43 member states currently owe the AU membership payments, Ethiopia is not only one of 11 AU member states that have fully paid their contributions for 2013, but also one of five that have made advance payments. In addition to the assessed annual financial contributions to the AU, Ethiopia has provided the land and buildings where the AU is hosted, and also offered all the human and physical facilities the OAU required in its earliest days.

Addis Ababa hosts the permanent representatives of AU member states and other states, the accredited diplomatic missions of the United States, the European Union (EU), China, India, Brazil and other countries, as well as the United Nations agencies and other international multilateral and humanitarian organisations. The US and EU each have two heads of delegations, an ambassador to Ethiopia and a permanent representative to the AU. The number of foreign diplomatic representatives can be expected to increase in the near future. Addis Ababa hosts many ministerial and presidential conferences, and the AU summit attracts an average of 7,000 diplomatic delegates, of whom more than 40 are heads of state.[4] The headquarters of the East African Standby Brigade are also in Ethiopia, which contributes troops to the brigade.

This paper argues that the role and influence of Ethiopia in IGAD, the AU and even at a global level was boosted by Emperor Haile Selassie and the late Ethiopian Prime Minister Meles Zenawi, two leaders with diametrically different leadership attributes. While the role played by Haile Selassie stems from the history of Ethiopia and its strong anti-colonial and anti-apartheid position, his charismatic personality and his reign of 40 years, the late prime minister's role had more to do with his personal competence, his two decades in office and his alliances with both the West and the East. Both men managed to play very important roles on the international platform while facing stiff resistance at home and accusations that their governments had a bad record on human rights. How did they manage to exude such confidence at regional and international levels without the same degree of internal support? In this regard, the paper explains how the intellectual competence, powers of persuasion, pan-African disposition,

---

3.   Federal Democratic Republic of Ethiopia, The Foreign Affairs and National Security Policy and Strategy, Ministry of Information, Press and Audiovisual Department, November 2002, Addis Ababa. Available at http://www.mfa.gov.et/resdoc.php?cpg=2 (accessed 2 November 2012), p. 107.

4.   Interview with Ministry of Foreign Affairs of Ethiopia, 12 April 2012.

personal ambition and the trust a leader enjoys among his peers and the international community will determine the role and influence a country may have on the AU. It argues that leaders significantly augment the influence a country enjoys in these regional and global governance institutions. Accordingly, the article argues that as the late prime minister enjoyed huge influence in the AU, IGAD and global forums, Ethiopia's influence has significantly increased in the past eight years or so.

By focusing on post-Meles Ethiopia, this article also questions whether Ethiopia's new leadership has the will and capacity to maintain or change the role of Ethiopia in the AU and IGAD. In this regard, the new leadership of Ethiopia under Prime Minister Haliemariam Desalgne will be seriously challenged in trying to fill the large diplomatic shoes of the late prime minister. Irrespective of the personalities of its leaders, Ethiopia's influence in IGAD and the AU will continue to grow due to its history, large population, strategic location, military strength and promising economic performance in recent times. In conclusion, the paper argues that, in order to maintain the influential position of Ethiopia in the AU and IGAD, in addition to filling the regional and global gap left by the late prime minister, the new leadership has to maintain not only extraordinary delivery of development services, but also to significantly improve democratic and human rights situation, without which maintenance of power will prove much more difficult than before.

Ethiopia's role in the OAU and its transformation into the AU

The end of the Cold War offered African leaders an opportunity to seek African solutions to various African problems. In the early 1990s, Africa experienced civil wars in the Democratic Republic of Congo (DRC), Liberia, Sierra Leone, Burundi, Central African Republic and Guinea-Bissau. Genocide in Rwanda; state failure in Somalia; and secessionist movements in Sudan also became real challenges to the African leadership, new and old, demanding urgent attention and action. African conflicts became more intra-state and less inter-state with localised manifestation and coverage, rather than civil wars that engulfed an entire country. As a result, Africa witnessed three times as many internally displaced persons (IDPs) as refugees. The humanitarian crises in Somalia[5] and Darfur[6] were the worst, with more than 300,000 deaths and 4.7 million IDPs

---

5.   Mehari Taddele Maru (2008), The Future of Somalia's Legal System and Its Contribution to Peace and Development, *Journal of Peace Building and Development*, Vol. 4, No. 1, Centre for Global Peace, American University. Available from http://pascal.library.american. edu:8083/ojs/index.php/jpd/article/view/109/117 (accessed 12 March 2011).

6.   Mehari Taddele Maru (2011), The Kampala Convention and its Contribution to International Law, *Journal of Internal Displacement*, Vol. 1, No. 1. Also available from http://journalinternaldisplacement.webs.com/announcements.htm (accessed 28 November 2011).

and refugees.[7] To meet these challenges, the institutional transformation of the OAU into the AU began with the declaration of the OAU extraordinary summit of heads of state and government in September 1999 in Sirte, Libya. Indicative of its purpose was the title and theme of the summit, "Strengthening OAU Capacity to enable it to meet the Challenges of the New Millennium," specifically by amending the OAU Charter to enhance the efficiency and effectiveness of the body.[8] This extraordinary summit, and the later AU Constitutive Act, shifted the mission and vision of the OAU from being mainly an organisation for anti-colonial solidarity to becoming more interventionist and integrationist in the form of the AU. The conspicuous interventionist and integrationist normative and institutional frameworks of the AU mark its differences from the OAU.

Ethiopia's Influence in IGAD and AU

Generally speaking, countries impact the peace and security, economy and trade as well as social and political life of their immediately neighbouring countries and region. Practically, such influence varies from one country to another. Some countries influence their region more markedly than others. Countries such as Nigeria (in ECOWAS) and South Africa (in SADC) exercise an ominously hegemonic role, while others such as Ethiopia, Kenya, Ghana and Algeria have key and influential roles in their respective regions and beyond.

A country with a troubled internal political history and located in a region plagued by violent internal and external conflicts, historically Ethiopia has faced serious foreign aggression against its independence from Italy, Egypt and Britain. Arising from this history, Ethiopia tends to use multilateral solutions and institutions to pursue its interests and address its concerns. This has contributed to the fact that the Horn of Africa, unlike the other regions, remains free of the fear of being dominated by a single country. Consequently, with the exception of some glitches related either to support provided to rebel or terrorist groups, Ethiopia enjoys peaceful relations with Kenya, Djibouti, South Sudan and the Republic of Sudan. Ethiopia has experienced security threats from its neighbours, particularly Somalia, Egypt and its former northern region, Eritrea. Since the time of Siad Barre's regime and the border war of 1977, Ethiopia has been

---

7.   Report of the United Kingdom House of Commons International Development Committee, *Darfur, Sudan and The Responsibility to protect*, 30 March 2005; Death in Darfur: The Story Behind the Numbers. Enough Project (26 January 2010); Internal Displacement Monitoring Centre (IDMC) (2009), *Internal Displacement, Global Overview of Trends and Developments in 2008*. Geneva: Norwegian Refugee Council, pp. 41–9. Available from http://www.internal-displacement.org/8025708F004CE90B/(httpPages)/22FB1D4E2B19 6DAA802570BB005E787C?OpenDocument&count=1000 (accessed 21 January 2013).

8.   African Union Summit, Transition from the OAU to the African Union. Available at http:// www.au2002.gov.za/docs/background/oau_to_au.htm (last visited 11 August 2012).

the victim of terrorist attacks and Jihad declarations from the violently extremist Somalian movements Al Itihad Al Islamyia and the Union of Islamic Courts as well as Al Shabaab. Ethiopia has been in a state of war with Eritrea since the 1998 border conflict. The rivalry with Egypt over the Nile has also destabilised Ethiopia for a long time and has increased the threats to its peace and development. Thus, Ethiopia understands that peace and security in the region are best achieved through collective regional and international mechanisms.

Ethiopia's contributions to Peace and Security in Africa and Beyond

Since the establishment of the UN and later the OAU and AU, Ethiopia has successfully participated in ten peacekeeping missions at continental and global level. As discussed above, Ethiopia is one of the staunchest supporters of the AU's new intervention and integration agenda. It currently has close to 7,000 troops in various UN peacekeeping missions, including with the United Nations Interim Security Force in Abyei (UNISFA). This makes Ethiopia one of the top five troop-contributing countries at both African and global levels. In the 1950s and 1960s, Ethiopia successfully participated in the UN peacekeeping missions in Korea and the Congo. More recently, Ethiopia also successfully participated in missions in Rwanda, Burundi and Liberia and Darfur, Sudan as well as Abyei. Ethiopia's peacekeepers have a good continental and global reputation.[9]

The country's engagement in peace mediation under the OAU began in 1972 with the Addis Ababa agreement signed under the auspices of Emperor Haile Selassie between the Government of Sudan (GoS) and rebel groups in South Sudan. Ethiopia, through IGAD and bilaterally, contributed significantly to the signing and implementation of the comprehensive peace agreement. This agreement was the result of exhausting and lengthy dispute settlement efforts by the AU, IGAD, the UN, the US and the European Union (EU). In continuation of its role in the IGAD region, Ethiopia had an influence on the peaceful referendum and independence of South Sudan.

---

9.   Born of the experience of victimisation, its struggle to maintain its independence and to demonstrate its convictions about collective security, Ethiopia, as one of the first signatories of the UN Charter, has been at the forefront of peacekeeping efforts in Africa and beyond. The common defence of Africa against any military aggression was also in the minds of Ethiopia's leaders. Ethiopia supported the proposed establishment of an African defence force similar to the current AU Standby Force. Emperor Haile Selassie warned African leaders not to "rely solely on international morality. Africa's control over her own affairs is dependent on the existence of appropriate military arrangements to assure this continent's protection against such threats. While guarding our own independence, we must at the same time determine to live peacefully with all nations of the world" Mehari Taddele Maru, (2012), *"The Contributions of Ethiopia to the Abyei Peacekeeping Force"*, Institute for Security Studies, ISS Today, available http://www.iss.co.za/iss_today.php?ID=1358 (accessed 31 March 2013, p.2.).

Currently, it has a crucial part in maintaining peace in the region. It serves as a trusted peacekeeping partner in the border areas of South Sudan and Sudan and is playing a vital role in the process to build a viable state in South Sudan. Facilitated by Thabo Mbeki, chief of AU's high-level implementation panel and a close friend of Meles Zenawi, the Addis agreement on Abyei was signed by the Sudan People's Liberation Movement (SPLM) forces and the government of Sudan in Addis Ababa on 20 June 2011. The main objective of the agreement is to ensure that this border area remains demilitarised until proper demarcation is undertaken. The same agreement provides for the deployment of UNISFA under UN Security Council Resolution 1990.[10]

UNISFA is composed of 4,250 Ethiopian troops, includes civilian police and is unique for many reasons. Unlike most peacekeeping missions, UNISFA is a mono-troop contingent of Ethiopian peacekeeping troops. The force commander, Ethiopian Lieutenant-General Taddesse Worede, and now Major General Yohannes Gebre Meskel, is also head of the mission. The deployment was swift compared to other peacekeeping missions. Under normal circumstances, troop deployment takes a long time, as potential troop-contributing countries need to be persuaded, and resources mobilised before the force can be deployed. UNISFA was deployed on 22 July 2011, a month after the authorisation of the mission by the United Nations Security Council through Resolution 1990 of 25 June 2011. Resolution 1990 was also passed swiftly, three days after the conclusion of the Addis agreement on Abyei on 20 June 2011, in terms of which the contending parties, the governments of Sudan and South Sudan, requested the deployment of Ethiopian peacekeeping troops. The request by the AU and UN as well as IGAD to Ethiopia to send troops to Abyei indicates the confidence of the international community in Ethiopia.

The main challenges to UNISFA and indirectly Ethiopia are keeping the balance between the two parties while maintaining their confidence. While this peacekeeping duty is undertaken on behalf of the international community and the UN, UNISFA could be deployed solely because of the trust both parties have in Ethiopia. Thus, for Ethiopia UNISFA is not a usual peacekeeping mission, but also an extra burden on its foreign policy relations with both neighbouring countries. Falling out of favour with either party will adversely affect UNISFA and Ethiopia's foreign relations. As time goes without determination of the status of Abyei and the fundamental political changes on the ground, Ethiopia may face more challenges in maintaining this balanced relations with both parties.

---

10. United Nations Security Council Resolution 1990, S/SER/2024 (2011), 14 December 2011. Available from http://www.un.org/en/peacekeeping/missions/unisfa/ (accessed January 21, 2012).

Ethiopia in IGAD

Ethiopia is one of very few African countries that belongs to a single regional economic community, namely IGAD. Thus, Ethiopian influence in the AU must also be seen in the context of its membership of IGAD. Most of its important initiatives on peace and security in the Horn of Africa are advanced and implemented through IGAD and pass to the AU indirectly. Ethiopia's influence on the AU reflects its role in IGAD. Under the rotational chairmanship, Sudan should have been the chair of IGAD. Due to the indictment of Sudanese President Omar Al Bashir, Sudan is unable to assume the position. By default, Ethiopia has been elected chair of IGAD for the past six years.

Ethiopian's influence in global and regional diplomatic circles, including the UN and the AU, has also contributed to its using multilateral mechanisms to pursue its interests. Excellent examples in this regard are Ethiopia's initiatives of sanctions against Eritrea and the post facto approval by the AU and the international community of its rather unpopular but effective intervention in Somalia. The Security Council sanctions were based on recommendations from IGAD approved by the AU.[11] Ethiopia has also played a critical role in the establishment of the Transitional Federal Government of Somalia (TFG) in Kenya following a peace process under the auspices of IGAD, the AU and the UN. The establishment of the TFG was facilitated by IGAD in 2004, while the AU Mission in Somalia (AMISOM) was first spearheaded by IGAD as an IGAD Mission in Somalia and only later the AU. With the backing of Ethiopian troops and subsequently AMISOM, TFG forces defeated the Islamic Courts at the end of 2006. AMISOM was authorised after the withdrawal of the Ethiopian army from Somalia in 2007. The 2011 incursions by the Ethiopian and Kenyan armies into the buffer areas in Somalia and the later re-hatting of the Kenyan army as AMISOM have helped the anti-Shabaab forces to expand their areas of control despite security and administrative vacuum. This has also assisted in the election of a new president and new parliament and in creating the present optimistic situation in Somalia.

Moreover, by maintaining the balance and playing the role of trusted arbiter, Ethiopia has become the fulcrum on which the balance of regional peace is maintained. For example, in the South Sudan/Sudan conflict, Uganda declared it would join South Sudan if the latter was attacked by Sudan. This shows that IGAD will not be able to constrain some countries from engaging in regional war. It also means that without the influential role of Ethiopia, IGAD member

11. UN Monitoring Group on Somalia and Eritrea, Letter from the Chairman of the Security Council Committee pursuant to resolutions 751 (1992) and 1907 (2009) concerning Somalia and Eritrea, UNSC S/2011/433, 18 July 2011.

states may not have the power they need. Eritrea, Djibouti, Kenya and Somalia may not be able to constrain Uganda in the way Ethiopia can.

In demonstration of its influence in regional and global diplomatic platforms, in all cases Ethiopia used the IGAD decision-making process to request the AU and Security Council to take decisions on Somalia, Eritrea and the conflict between the two Sudans in line with its foreign policies.

Ethiopia and African Integration

Since the inception of the OAU and later the AU, Ethiopia has been cautiously optimistic and supportive of the integrationist project.[12] Ethiopia currently prioritises integration within regional economic communities, specifically IGAD, as a first step towards continent-wide integration. It pursues a gradualist, practical integration, beginning with the development of these regional communities and with a focus on the economic and market integration of the continent.[13] In recent years, Ethiopia has better infrastructural links with Sudan and Djibouti and similar links are being constructed with Kenya, South Sudan and Somalia. Ethiopia has also begun exporting electricity to Djibouti and Sudan, and intends to do so with Kenya, Somaliland, South Sudan and Egypt. Ethiopia, Africa's second-most populous country and already the preeminent player in peace and security in IGAD, appears poised to become a regional economic engine.[14] It is placing more emphasis on infrastructural linkages among these countries and complementary tradeamong the economies of the countries undergoing integration.

Ethiopia's position on integration is in direct contradiction of the position of the late Colonel Muammar Qaddafi and his supporters on the immediate establishment of the United States of Africa.[15] The sudden metamorphosis of Colonel Qaddafi from lead promoter of Arab unity to advocate and financier of the United States of Africa can only be explained by his frustration with the League of Arab States and his personal ambition to become a leader of the United States of Africa. To use African affairs in the service of his private inter-

12. Molefi Asante (2012), The Character of Kwame Nkrumah's United Africa Vision, *Journal of Pan Africa Studies*, Vol. 4, No. 10, January.

13. Otchere-Darko, Asare (2007), "And Gaddafi Shifted", *AU Monitor*. Available at http://www.pambazuka.org/aumonitor/comments/268/ (accessed 21 January 2013).

14. William Davison (2011), "Ethiopia begins electricity exports to neighbouring Djibouti, utility says", *Bloomberg*, 10 June. Available from http://www.bloomberg.com/news/2011-06-10/ethiopia-begins-electricity-exports-to-neighboring-djibouti-utility-says.html (accessed 21 January 2013); Tesfa-Alem Tekle (2011), "Ethiopia: Power Network links to Sudan, Djibouti Finalized", *Sudan Tribune*, 25 April. Available from http://www.sudantribune.com/Ethiopia-Power-network-links-to,38687 (accessed 21 January 2013).

15. Christian Lowe (2010), "We can build United States of Africa, Gaddafi says", *Reuters*, 27 July. Available from http://www.reuters.com/article/2010/07/27/us-africa-summit-gaddafi-idUSTRE66Q70620100727 (accessed 21 January 2013).

ests, he flooded the AU and some leaders with cash. Colonel Qaddafi widely introduced what a former permanent representative of Nigeria to the AU dubbed "envelope diplomacy."[16] He also built gas stations, mosques and hotels in many African countries. Libya, like South Africa, Nigeria, Egypt and Algeria, not only contributed annually 15 per cent (around US$ 16 million) of the AU's budget, but also covered the expenses of many smaller and poorer African countries and funded many AU events, including ordinary and extraordinary AU summits. Accordingly, Ethiopia took a strong stand against Colonel Qaddafi's urge to integrate Africa from the top down, which Ethiopia and other African countries believed was unrealistic. Colonel Qaddafi began his futile and again impracticable efforts to move the headquarters of the AU from Addis Ababa to Sirte at the early inception of the AU early in 1999. When this failed, Colonel Qaddafi strove to host most of the summits in Libya. In doing so, he tried to make his hometown Sirte the *de facto* seat of the AU by building brand new facilities.

The AU rules governing the hosting of summits stipulates Addis Ababa, the headquarters of the AU, hosts the January/February summit every year. However, individual member states can request the AU to allow them to host the June/July summit. This regional rotation and having two summits per year was originally devised in response to pressure from Colonel Qaddafi and as a compromise.[17] Because of his destructive interventions in many African countries, including his support for Idi Amin of Uganda, 1980 intervention in Chad, support for rebel groups in Eritrea, Somalia, Sudan, Niger, Mali, Sierra Leone and Liberia[18] and his unrealistic integration agenda as well as his limitless personal interests, Qaddafi's "conversion" from Pan-Arab to Pan African leader was not taken at face value. His immediate integrationist agenda was propagated without Libya ratifying the AU treaties that required minimal action towards integration and strictly limiting mobility of people to Libya from other African countries. When his grand plan of making Sirte the AU capital and of establishing a United States of Africa under his leadership failed, Colonel Qaddafi established and funded the Community of Sahel-Saharan States (CEN-SAD), which grew into a bloc of 28 African states. Designed to serve as an alternative means of achieving his grand plan, CEN-SAD, like his other initiatives, was used as a tool to "blackmail." Even though he invited Ethiopia and Uganda several times, they were the only two IGAD member states that refused to join CEN-SAD.

Since the establishment of the AU in 2002, Ethiopia along with Nigeria, South Africa and Uganda formed a bulwark against Qaddafi's unrealistic plans

---

16. Interview with former Nigerian permanent representative to the AU who attended last OAU summits, 11 April 2012.
17. Ibid.
18. Adekeye Adebajo (2011), "Gaddafi: the man who would be king of Africa", *The Guardian*, 26 August. Available from www.guardian.co.uk (accessed 9 November 2012).

and ambitions. In most of the AU summits, former Nigerian President Oluse-gun Obasanjo acted as diplomatic intermediary, as did the former South Afri-can President Thabo Mbeki and late Ethiopian Prime Minister Meles Zenawi. Ugandan President Yoweri Museveni also strongly opposed the ambitions of Colonel Qaddafi. Dancing to the tune of Libyan dinars, some leaders such as Abdoulaye Wade of Senegal voted in support of proposals of Colonel Qaddafi. Prime Minister Meles and President Museveni remained at the forefront of the bloc against Qaddafi when Obasanjo and Mbeki left office.

During the uprisings in Libya, Ethiopia, Nigeria and Sudan took the most progressive positions against Colonel Qaddafi. Based on national and person-al interests, they supported the legitimate aspirations of the Libyan people.[19] Ethiopia aggressively advocated the end of Colonel Qaddafi's regime.[20] Sudan exhibited even more aggression than others by sending its troops and military support to the National Transitional Council (NTC). This was considered as revenge for Colonel Qaddafi's support for many rebel groups in Darfur and elsewhere in the Sudan.[21] In a long debate at the AU summit in Malabo in July 2011, Ethiopia's position was vehemently opposed by South Africa and other countries, mainly on the basis of a common voice against external interven-tion by NATO in Libya.[22] The AU, led by South Africa and its President Jacob Zuma, decided not to recognise the NTC even after Tripoli fell under its con-trol. Ethiopia and Nigeria issued a joint communiqué in support of recognising the NTC. This was a significant contribution by Ethiopia to facilitate AU sup-port to end the Libyan uprisings.

Currently, there is an opportunity for sombre and realistic leadership in de-livering the promises of the AU. As I have argued elsewhere:

> [W]ithout a doubt, the foreign policy and relations of the NTC and the fu-ture elected Libyan government will be different from that of Gaddafi. Firstly, Gaddafi's foreign policy in Africa stems from his individualistic interest to lead a United States of Africa – a project in which he has heavily, but unsuccessfully, invested for the last decade. Libya was too small a territory and population for "the Brother Leader". He needed a much bigger territory and population to lead. For the NTC, and presumably for the next elected government, Libya will still be

---

19. Mehari Taddele Maru (2011) How the AU Should Have Recognized the Libyan NTC, *ISS Today*. Available from http://www.iss.co.za/iss_today.php?ID=1348 (accessed 28 Novem-ber 2011).

20. Mehari Taddele Maru (2011) On Unconstitutional Changes of Government: The Case of Libya, *ISS Today*. Available from http://www.iss.co.za/iss_today.php?ID=1358 (accessed 28 November 2012).

21. *Tripoli Post* (2o11), "Sudan supported NTC Forces in the fight against Al Qathafi", 27 October. Available from www.tripolipost.com (accessed 28 January 2013).

22. Interview with former Malian permanent representative to the AU who attended Malabo AU summits, 11 April 2012.

a challenge to govern, given that some of the clans may think of establishing their own "emirates". That is the reason why the AU is concerned about the territorial integrity of Libya.[23]

Libya's current internal situation and disposition reduce the likelihood of its playing the role it did during Colonel Qaddafi's rule. This reflects the incongruity between the priorities of the Libyan people and those of its former leader. At the same time, the AU should consider the implications of the possible withdrawal of Libya's 15 per cent budget contribution. Moreover, with the absence of Colonel Qaddafi from AU summits, proponents of the gradual integration favoured by the late Prime Minister Meles Zenawi have gained the upper hand in the debate.[24]

Given current economic determinants and the lack of complementary trade and economic linkages among countries, integration remains an excellent aspiration but lacks the elements required for implementation. Indeed, without the mobilisation of the trade and economic drivers of integration, such as free mobility of goods, services, capital and people, integration is unthinkable. The vital steps towards integration should be creating an enabling policy environment in Africa through free movement protocols, fewer tariffs and the implementation of most of the common market treaties such as the Common Market for Eastern and Southern Africa (COMESA) and the East African Community (EAC).

Role of Leaders

Notwithstanding the size of a country, leaders can and have achieved for their countries regional power status out of proportion to the material power, economy, military or other kinds of power those countries actually have. Personal motivation and the competence of the leader and his/her pan-African inclinations and ambitions are driving factors in the contribution a country can make to and the influence it can have on the AU. Former Nigerian President Olusegun Obasanjo, former South African President Thabo Mbeki, John Kufuor, Emperor Haile Selassie and Meles Zenawi played more prominent roles than most of their immediate predecessors or successors on account of their individual leadership skills, their intellectual competence and their pan-African commitment. Their long-term incumbency also allowed them to shape the AU agenda.

As mentioned above, Rwanda and Burundi have contributed significantly to peace and security in Sudan and Somalia, while Colonel Qaddafi of Libya, a small but economically strong country, was prominent on African platforms. He

23. Mehari Taddele Maru (2011), How the AU Should Have Recognized the Libyan NTC, *ISS Today*. Available from http://www.iss.co.za/iss_today.php?ID=1348 (accessed 28 November 2011).
24. Robert Nolan (2011), The African Union After Gaddafi, *Journal of Diplomacy*, [Vol. 2 No.1]. Available from http://blogs.shu.edu/diplomacy/2011/12/the-african-union-after-gaddafi/ (accessed 21 January 2013).

was the man behind the United States of Africa agenda. Regardless of the size of the country, personal capacity and the pan-African inclinations of a leader are critical in the securing of peace and security. Olusegun Obasanjo in Nigeria is another example in the whole gamut of leadership. Of course, Nigeria is a large country, but, in regard to the AU and ECOWAS, his personal stand and vision for the AU was more important, since he is a committed pan-Africanist whose policy was to treat African issues as a national priority. Under his leadership, Nigeria led many mediation and peacekeeping efforts in Africa. By contrast, for various reasons his successor Umaru Yar'Adua was nowhere evident in regional dynamics. In the same vein, Thabo Mbeki was more popular in AU circles than in South Africa and showed more pan-African leadership and engagement than Jacob Zuma. The latter was and remains at odds with many African leaders and the policies of the AU, ranging from the issue of Côte d'Ivoire to Somalia. Likewise, John Kufuor of Ghana was a more active pan-African leader than the late John Atta Mills.

Ethiopia's direct financial contribution to the AU is only US$ 1.5 million per annum, less than one-tenth of each of the biggest five contributing countries, Nigeria, South Africa, Egypt, Algeria and Libya. Ethiopia's unmatched contributions to the OAU/AU are rooted not only in Ethiopia's historical role as a seedbed for pan-African movements, but also the unwavering commitment of its leaders to pan-African causes. Despite the serious resistance and challenges they faced in their governance at home, the leaders of Ethiopia, particularly Emperor Haile Selassie and Prime Minister Meles Zenawi, amplified the influence of Ethiopia beyond its economic and military strength. While there is congruity between general domestic public opinion and Ethiopia's active role in the AU, nonetheless tensions remain between Ethiopia's internal governance issues and its leading role in the AU. How did Ethiopian leaders like the Prime Minister Zenawi managed to play such a key role on the international platform while facing stiff resistance at home on account of weak human rights records and for failing to ensure access to the sea during the secession of Eritrea from Ethiopia? This has to do more with their ability to exude influence and enjoy the confidence of global actors such as the AU/OAU and UN, and dominant powers such as the US, the EU and China.

The late Meles Zenawi increased the role and influence of Ethiopia in IGAD, the AU and even at a global level as a result of three main factors. First, he stayed in power for two decades as president and prime minister and was influential in politics for almost four decades. Second, the AU, IGAD and the international community found him to be intelligent in proposing solutions for complicated issues and persuasive and competent in advocating African positions at global forums such as the G20 and G8, climate change forums, New Partnership for Africa's Development (NEPAD) sessions, and so on. One significant contribution to the AU was Ethiopia's chairing of NEPAD for almost a decade since January 2007. Similarly, the late prime minister was the voice of Africa on the Forum for China-Africa Cooperation (FOCAC) and in partnerships with India and South Korea. Ethiopia's involvement in these various forums is strongly rooted in the philosophy of its internal policy, which prioritises eradication of poverty and the achievement of the Millennium Development Goals (MDGs). As a result of these engagements, the prime minister acted as de facto chairperson of the AU.

His influence in diplomatic circles also helped him in the successful diplomatic pursuit of Ethiopia's interests and the maintenance of his government in power. Excellent examples in this regard are Ethiopia's diplomatic victory against Eritrea and its position on Somalia and the Sudan that are supported by the AU and the international community.

Quest for New Causes of Solidarity: Re-defining Pan Africanism for the 21st Century

The transformation of the OAU into the AU in a way represented an attempt to answer the quest for new causes African solidarity and to redefine pan-Africanism. Based on the AU Constitutive Act, the first AU Commission strategic plan declared that the vision of the AU is "to build an integrated, a prosperous and peaceful Africa, driven by its own citizens and representing a dynamic force in the international arena".[25] The shift from collective security of states to human security was articulated in detail in the Constitutive Act, the strategic plans and in various other instruments, mainly the African Peace and Security Architecture (APSA) and NEPAD.

Having the ultimate purpose of eradicating violent conflict and poverty from Africa, APSA and NEPAD took pride of place in the work of the AU and as part of the AU architecture to eradicate poverty and secure development. Through this architecture, the AU and its member states endorsed the MDGs. The AU Constitutive Act, APSA, AGA and NEPAD can be considered primarily as new milestones and as an unofficial attempt to re-define pan-Africanism in an era of intervention and integration.

One important difference between the OAU and AU is the latter's right to intervene[26] in a member state to prevent any grave circumstances arising, namely,

---

25. AU Commission (2004) *Commission of the African Union: 2004–2007 Strategic Plan*, Vol. 2 Strategic Framework, May, pp. 1–2.

26. Article 4(h) of the Constitutive Act stipulates "the right of the Union to intervene in a Member State pursuant to a decision of the Assembly in respect of grave circumstances, namely war crimes, genocide and crimes against humanity" and Article 4 (j) refers to the "the right of Member States to request intervention from the Union in order to restore peace and security." These formulations are put as a "right" and not an "obligation." Nonetheless, they are conceived of as the duty of the AU and member states when grave circumstances prevail in another member state.

war crimes, genocide and crimes against humanity, as well as to secure peace and order in a region.[27] The shift in the mission of the AU lays on its success in combining three elements: 1) the sovereignty of member states, 2) their responsibility to protect their nationals, and 3) African solidarity expressed by the duty of the AU to assist states with grave internal crises to meet their duty to protect nationals. The AU may intervene in a member state when an internal crisis takes the form of war crimes, genocide and crimes against humanity. These considerations distinguish intervention from interference.

The benefits of this conception are significant.[28] In the past ten years, the AU has responded to urgent crises in Somalia, Darfur, South Sudan, Côte d'Ivoire, Madagascar, Niger, Mauritania, Mali and the recent popular uprisings in North Africa, albeit with varying degrees of success. The signing of the comprehensive peace agreement between the government of Sudan and SPLM in 2005 and the Darfur peace agreement between Darfuri rebel groups and the Sudanese government were examples of success. The AU's High-Level Implementation Panel on Sudan (AUHIP) remains one of the most active peace mechanisms. Without such engagement from the AU and other international and sub-regional actors, the probable cost of the pre-and post-referendum situation in South Sudan would have been enormous. The AU-UN Hybrid Mission in Darfur (UNAMID), predecessor of the AU Mission in Sudan (AMIS), has improved the situation on the ground. The AU Mission in Somalia (AMISOM), an entirely AU peacekeeping mission, has since August 2011 significantly improved the prospects for peace and security through its tireless efforts to bring Somalia out of its statelessness. In addition, regional economic communities such as ECOWAS, IGAD and SADC have become active in the AU's interventionist and integrationist agenda.[29]

A less remarked characteristic of the era of intervention and integration is

---

27. The AU Constitutive Act of the African Union, OAU, 'Decision on the Establishment of the African Union and the Pan-African Parliament', AHG/Dec. 143(XXXVI).

28. Apart from AU-approved peacekeeping missions and other interventions, in terms of the newly adopted Kampala Convention on IDPs, the responsibility for addressing the plight of IDPs is placed on all states. In line with the principle of the responsibility to protect, the intervention duty of international and regional mechanisms such as the AU mandate to intervene is clearly stipulated. In accordance with the principle of subsidiarity, the Kampala Convention reinforces the power of the AU to intervene for protection purposes in a manner compatible with the AU Constitutive Act and international law.

29. The regional economic communities have robustly exercised the right of intervention in the maintenance of peace and security in Africa: ECOWAS in Liberia, Sierra Lone, Côte d'Ivoire, Niger and Mauritania; IGAD in Somalia, South Sudan and Darfur; and SADC in Burundi, Zimbabwe and Madagascar. Peace and Security Council deliberations also focused on the Central African Republic, the Democratic Republic of Congo, Chad, Comoros, and Côte d'Ivoire, Burundi and Mauritania. The AU has been actively involved in monitoring elections in Africa, and subsequently, in mediation efforts when post-election violence occurred in many African countries. In this regard, the AU was busy in Kenya (2007), Zimbabwe (2008), Côte D'Iovire (2010), Mali (2012) and Guinea-Bissau (2012).

the profile of Africa's leaders. The first AU summits were composed of long-serving dictators, some of them, such as Robert Mugabe, the leaders of former independence liberation movements. Other AU leaders, such as Yoweri Museveni, were new generation rebel rulers who waged decades of civil war to topple military dictators. In addition, there were democratically elected leaders such as Thabo Mbeki. Since then, we have witnessed political struggles to extend constitutional terms of office and many countries have held elections that were marred by election-rigging and post-election disputes and violence. The results were fragmented political parties and mandates, in contrast to grand coalitions and smooth transfers of power in countries like Kenya and Zimbabwe. Despite all these problems, since the establishment of the AU we have seen more than 35 countries hold democratic elections, half of which resulted in a peaceful take-over of power by victorious opposition parties.[30]

Nevertheless, the North African uprisings reveal the vulnerability of Africa to revolution and violence, phenomena that are symptomatic of the undemocratic nature of states, the illegitimate exercise of power, as well as the weakness of peaceful and constitutional avenues to change government. The slow but comparatively well formulated response of the AU to the uprisings exposed the deficiencies and impotence of the AU in challenging the leadership of people such as Colonel Qaddafi, who ruled for decades without legitimacy of any kind. The uprising initiated useful introspection about the need for the AU to insist on democratic reform and peaceful democratic transition. By failing to demand democratic governance reform in countries such as Libya, Africa and the AU by default allowed external military forces to intervene.

More terribly, the AU missed an opportunity to be the primary promoter of democracy and driver of democratic transformation in Africa. With the North African uprisings, the generational progression towards democratisation has been accelerated. With the era of lifelong rule waning fast, the next generation believes one or two terms in office is long enough to deliver election promises and make the necessary impact on the society. Democracy without delivery of good governance services poses serious challenges for social stability, while service delivery without democracy devalues human dignity and diminishes the capacity for growth. A vital message and deterrent particularly to newly elected and emerging political leaders is that power solely dependent on performance in delivering services would be difficult to sustain. Accordingly, the AU needs to identify new frontiers of pan-Africanism for the 21st Century. This Pan-Afri-

30. Mehari Taddele Maru (2012), *Salient Features of the 18th African Union Summit: Generational Progression Democracy in Africa.* Available from http://studies.aljazeera.net/en/reports/2012/02/20122111410505510.htm (accessed 4 February 2012).

canism should stem from poverty eradication and democratisation by providing states with the capacity to deliver and democratise more.

Conclusion

Ethiopia's place in the AU is entrenched in its historical role as seedbed of African history, its support to the anti-colonial and apartheid struggle and its critical role in the establishment of the OAU and AU. Signifying the country's genuine commitment to the cause of the OAU and AU, successive rulers of Ethiopia have continued to pursue the same foreign policy towards both bodies. Rooted in its history and heavily dependent on the pan-African disposition and calibre of its leaders, Ethiopia's current meaningful influence in the AU, however, flows from its leading role in IGAD and in diplomatic successes in international forums. Nonetheless, Ethiopia's commitment to the AU's ideals and values as expressed in the various AU and OAU normative instruments, falters when it comes to its own internal governance. Ethiopia has yet to ratify and implement more than 15 conventions (35 per cent) of the total of 43 binding AU instruments. To its credit, Ethiopia ratified the African Charter on Democracy, Elections and Governance within a year of its adoption. The treaties awaiting ratification include the Protocol of the African Court of Justice, the Protocol on the Statute of the African Court of Justice and Human Rights, the African Youth Charter, the African Union Convention for the Protection and Assistance of Internally Displaced Persons in Africa (the Kampala Convention), the African Charter on Values and Principles of Public Service and Administration, the Convention on the Conservation of Nature and Natural Resources and the Non-Aggression and Common Defence Pact. These instruments are vital for ensuing human security in Ethiopia and in enabling the state to deliver and democratise more.

Currently, African countries, including Ethiopia, have progressive legislative and institutional frameworks but anachronistically regressive, oppressive and manipulative practices. These treaties are like the clothes that are hanging in a closet, but which need to be worn and integrated into the real life of African states and African people. Ratification is meaningless if treaties are not domesticated and implemented. Once ratified, implementation remains a challenge.[31]

Ethiopia, Africa's second-most populous country and the region's key political player, with a long history of Pan-African solidarity and contributions to international and African peace and security, has significant influence on the AU. Nonetheless, Ethiopia will enjoy more influence by first ratifying the 15 instruments it is expected to implement. And, as the seat of the AU headquarters, Ethiopia should offer an enabling environment and platforms for pan-

---

31. List of countries that have signed, ratified/acceded to the AU instruments, 2010, available from http://www.au.int/en/treaties/status (accessed on 10 November 2011).

African state and non-state actors to enter the country without cumbersome visa requirements so as to create a space for pan-African debate on the AU agenda and pan-African monitoring of AU activities. In a nutshell, Ethiopia should be an example on all these counts.

Algeria and the African Union

From National Liberation Struggle to Fight against Terrorism[1]

Yahia H. Zoubir

Introduction

In the new millennium, Algeria has emerged as a key player in the so-called War on Terror and has become a central player in the African Union's (AU) anti-terrorism initiatives. This has not always been the case. Indeed, from independence in 1962 until the late 1970s, Algeria adopted a strong anti-imperialist stance. Within the Organisation of African Unity (OAU), Algeria focused on supporting national liberation movements, African unity and fairer global economic exchanges. Because of the legitimacy earned through their involvement in the fierce anti-colonial war against France, Algerian nationalists assumed a leadership role in the OAU. However, since the 1990s, Algeria has espoused its new role as leading actor in the so-called war against terrorism in order to regain the credibility in international relations lost in the intervening period.[2]

In order to explain Algeria's foreign policy shift, the article uses the Role Approach[3] to show the different conceptions of national role Algerian policy-makers adopted at different times. From the 1960s through to the early 1980s, Algeria played or sought to play the role of liberation supporter, regional leader,

---

1. Given the absence of writings on Algeria's role in the AU (the latest scholarly work on Algeria's Africa policy is Slimane Chikh. *L'Algérie porte de l'Afrique,* Algiers: Casbah, 1999), the author has relied on interviews with senior Algerian diplomats and with African leaders, notably Salim Ahmed Salim, the OAU Secretary-General from 1989 to 2001(interview Dar Salam, Tanzania, 5 September 2012) and other AU officials. Ambassador Ramtane Lamamra, AU Commissioner for Peace and Security, and Ambassador Saïd Djinnit, UNSG Special Representative for West Africa, provided invaluable insights. The author would also like to thank Linnéa Gelot, Mikael Eriksson and Rita Abrahamsen for their constructive comments on earlier drafts of this article.

2. Yahia H. Zoubir, "The Resurgence of Algeria's Foreign Policy in the Twenty-First Century," in Michael Bonner, Megan Reif, and Mark Tessler (eds), *Islam, Democracy, and the State in Algeria* (London: Routledge, 2005), pp. 16983.

3. According to Holsti, "a national role conception includes the policy-makers' own definitions of the general kinds of decisions, commitments, rules, and actions suitable to their state, and of the functions, if any, their state should perform on a continuing basis in the international system or in subordinate regional systems," K.J. Holsti: "National Role Conceptions in the Study of Foreign Policy," in Stephen G. Walker (ed.), *Role Theory and Foreign Policy Analysis* (Durham NC: Duke University Press, 1987), p. 12. See also Sofiane Sekhri, "The Role Approach as a Theoretical Framework for the Analysis of Foreign Policy in Third World Countries," *African Journal of Political Science and International Relations,* 3, 10 (October 2009):423–32; Lisbeth Aggestam ,"Role Conceptions and the Politics of Identity in Foreign Policy". Department of Political Science: University of Stockholm. ARENA *Working Papers,* 1999, available at: http://www.arena.uio.no/publications/wp99_8.htm

active independent, developer, and mediator. Since the late 1990s, Algeria's role was mainly as regional and anti-terrorist leader.[4] Such roles were meant to serve the country's core national interests and defined goals by exerting influence within regional and international institutions. When such core goals were not achieved (for instance, the failure to establish a New International Economic Order or NIEO or lessen dependency on the capitalist North), Algeria struggled to increase its importance as a driving force against international terrorism so as to gain support among the major powers, namely the United States and Europe.

Close analysis of Algeria's policy towards sub-Saharan Africa suggests it used the OAU to achieve its national interests and those of the entire continent. Today, the African Union (AU) serves as the platform from which Algeria seeks to effect its antiterrorist vision globally.

This article discusses Algeria's relations with the OAU and, since 2002, the AU. It proceeds in three stages to examine the various roles Algeria has played. The first part examines Algeria's relations with sub-Saharan Africa and with and within African institutions in general. As noted, until the early 1980s Algeria sought to sway the OAU to support its anti-imperialist and liberator roles. However, Algeria now focuses primarily on questions of peace and security, conflict resolution, as well as combating terrorism, without neglecting development issues. The second part of the article examines Algeria's response to and role in the perceived transnationalisation of the Sahel crisis. In the third part, recent developments in Mali serve as an illustration of the rationale for Algeria's foreign policy approach to Africa in recent years. The article concludes that Algeria has played out its national role rather successfully, as shown in the number of leadership positions held by Algerians in the OAU and AU, and in those pan-African organisations' endorsement of various Algerian-inspired proposals.

Africa in Algeria's Policy

To understand Algeria's relations with the AU, we have to consider the country's enduring relations with sub-Saharan Africa since the 1950s.[5] Besides relations with the Maghreb and Arab world, relations with sub-Saharan African countries and the OAU constituted one of the pillars of Algeria's foreign policy.[6] Well before the country's independence, the National Council of the Algerian Revolu-

---

4. Algerians feel their experience in fighting and defeating domestic terrorism enables them to legitimately claim expertise in the field and to share it with other nations willing to cooperate regionally and internationally.

5. Robert A. Mortimer, "The Algerian Revolution in Search of the African Revolution," *Journal of Modern African Studies,* 8, 3 (October 1970):363–87; Paul Balta, "La Politique africaine de l'Algérie," *Revue Française d'Etudes Politiques Africaines (RFEPA),* 132 (1976): 54–73.

6. Nicole Grimaud. *La politique extérieure de l'Algérie* (Paris : Karthala, 1984).

tion (CNRA), the supreme organ of the National Liberation Front (FLN) that guided the war against France, had established close ties with African liberation movements and decided to multiply and consolidate relations with newly independent African states and with the liberation movements.[7] During the war of independence against France, Algerian revolutionaries participated in all inter-African meetings. They secured solidarity with independent African states and tangible support from liberation movements fighting for independence. Algeria's own struggle for independence also served as an inspiration for other liberation movements on the continent and beyond.[8] Furthermore, the FLN secured positions of leadership in various Third World organisations, especially with the acceleration of the decolonisation that had begun in the mid-1950s.[9] Henceforth, the relationship that the nationalists established with various movements and governments in Africa and Asia allowed the Algerian question to be placed on the agenda of the UN General Assembly, where it gathered support among Afro-Asian and Latin American countries as of 1955, one year after the launching of the war against France.[10]

Barely a month before independence, the June 1962 Tripoli Programme clearly stated that Algeria's foreign policy objectives would be "concerted" and based on "total solidarity in the struggle against imperialism … support for national liberation movements … enlargement of the movement of struggle and reinforcement of the front for unity."[11] The programme left no doubt that solidarity with the Third World – sub-Saharan Africa in particular – and socialist nations, as well as progressive forces in Western countries, had two major objectives: allowing Algeria to "face its responsibilities on the international plane" and as "a necessary corollary to … our domestic objectives. It will allow our country to achieve the objectives of [the] Revolution and … participate in the creation of a new world." This commitment was reiterated in the 1976 National Charter and inscribed four months later in the 1976 Constitution: "The struggle against colonialism, neocolonialism, imperialism and racial discrimination,

---

7. Historic documents containing pronouncements of the Algerian revolutionaries can be found in, Mohammed Harbi. *Archives de la Révolution Algérienne* (Paris: Editions Jeune Afrique, 1981); Slimane Chikh. *L'Algérie porte de l'Afrique*, Algiers: Casbah, 1999, pp. 295–6.

8. Slimane Chikh, "L'Algérie et l'Afrique: 1954–1962," *Revue Algérienne des Sciences juridiques, politiques et économiques*, 3 (1968):703–46.

9. For pre-independence Algeria's participation in numerous Third World organisations where it secured solid support, see Chikh, "L'Algérie et l'Afrique: 1954–1962."

10. Marvin David Muhlhausen. *The Action of the United Nations in the Algerian Crisis* (Madison WI: University of Wisconsin, 1963).

11. Projet de Programme pour la réalisation de la révolution démocratique populaire (adoptée à l'unanimité par le CNRA à Tripoli en Juin 1962), available at: http://www.el-mouradia.dz/francais/symbole/textes/symbolefr.htm, accessed 16 November 2009.

constitutes a fundamental axis of the Revolution." The National Charter[12] made plain that to defeat neocolonialism and imperialism, Algeria would wage "a tireless struggle for a new world economic order and for a system of international relations that will guarantee the right of all states to have a say in the settlement of the outstanding problems of our time."[13] For Algerians, political liberation was not enough: there had also to be a "fight for economic liberation."[14] This, in turn, required "complete and unlimited sovereignty over natural resources"[15] through their nationalisation and the nationalisation of the means to develop them. This would obviously lead to "a battle for control of prices," but all these initiatives would be impossible without "worldwide solidarity of action by all exploited countries."[16] Until the "liberal" turn of the 1980s, Algerian diplomacy endeavoured to achieve these objectives, and the liberation of Africa became the favoured terrain for Algeria's diplomatic action and allowed Algeria to play an active role on the international stage.[17] Algeria offered financial, political and military support to a wide variety of African liberation movements[18] and played an important role within the OAU.

Algeria and the Organisation of African Unity (OAU)

Sub-Saharan Africa was one of Algeria's main backers in its anti-colonial war and played considerable role in shaping some of the Algerian ideas eventually adopted by the OAU. Algeria was one of the founding members of the organisation, which came into being on 25 May 1963.[19] One could argue, Algeria also grounded some of the OAU's early principles. The country's leaders used the OAU as the main forum to propagate a radical anti-colonial and anti-imperialist discourse that insisted on the total liberation of Africa.[20] Indeed, Algeria was one of the initial nine members of the OAU Liberation Committee, whose task was to raise and disburse funds to national liberation movements. Many of Algeria's

12. Democratic and Popular Algerian Republic. *National Charter* (Algiers: Ministry of Culture and Information, 1981).
13. *National Charter*, p. 97.
14. Ibid., p. 98.
15. Ibid.
16. Ibid.
17. Slimane Chikh, "La politique africaine de l'Algérie," in Hubert Michel and Maurice Flory (eds), *Annuaire de l'Afrique du Nord*, Vol. 17 (Paris : CNRS/CRESM, 1979):3. This article is one of the most thorough on Algeria's relations with Africa.
18. Many, including Nelson Mandela and other ANC members, received military training as well as political and financial support. Algeria supported several movements, such as the PAIGC (Guinea-Bissau), FRELIMO (Mozambique), MPLA (Angola), SWAPO (Namibia), ANC (South Africa) and ZAPU (Rhodesia), that eventually acceded to power.
19. See Creation of the OAU website, under "Biographies of the Founding Fathers," available at: http://www.oau-creation.com/The%20Biographies%20of%20the%20Founding%20Fathers.htm
20. Chikh, *La politique africaine de l'Algérie*, p. 15.

central Third World policies[21] were inscribed into the OAU Charter adopted at the first OAU meeting in 1963. Algeria's first president, Ahmed Ben Bella, gave a memorable anti-colonialist speech emphasising the liberation of the continent and the necessity for unity.[22] Algeria promoted and has been a staunch defender of two core OAU values: the inviolability of the borders inherited from the colonial era *uti possidetis* (a principle of international law that a territory remains with its owner at the end of a conflict), and non-interference by any member state in the internal affairs of another. These remain central to the AU's Charter,[23] even if the OAU policy of non-interference/non-intervention has shifted to the AU's commitment to "non-indifference,"[24] thus making the AU "the world's only regional or international organization that explicitly recognizes the right to intervene in a member state on humanitarian and human rights grounds."[25] One may also argue that the concept of inviolable borders has softened, as illustrated by AU support for the referendum in South Sudan. Be that as it may, Algerian policy-makers have steadfastly upheld these two principles, as was the case in 1967-1970 when they sided with Nigeria against the secessionist movement in Biafra. Today, they still refuse to contravene these two principles, which are inscribed in the Algerian constitution, even when national security warrants otherwise, as in the Libyan crisis of 2011 or the Malian crisis of 2012–13. In both cases, Algeria opposed foreign interference and in the second rejected the National Movement for the Liberation of the Azawad's (MNLA) proclamation in April 2012 of an independent state in northern Mali. As will be seen, Algeria's position on both crises was identical to the AU's, thus highlighting the country's continued influence within the regional organisation, but also of the continuity of some of Algeria's core foreign policy principles.[26]

---

21. Bahgat Korany, "Third Worldism and Pragmatic Radicalism: The Foreign Policy of Algeria," in Bahgat Korany and Ali E. Hillal Dessouki (eds), *The Foreign Policies of Arab States* (Boulder CO: Westview Press, 1984), pp. 79-118.

22. David B. Ottaway and Marina Ottaway, *Algeria: The Politics of a Socialist Revolution* (Stanford, CA: University of California Press, 1970), p. 163.

23. Article 4 (b) insists on the "Respect of borders existing on achievement of independence," while Article 4 (g) underlines "non-interference by any Member State in the internal affairs of another," http://www.au.int/en/sites/default/files/Constitutive_Act_en_0.htm

24. First AU Commissioner for Peace and Security Saïd Djinnit coined the notion of "non-indifference." See Kristina Powell, "The African Union's Emerging Peace and Security Regime: Opportunities and Challenges for Delivering on the Responsibility to Protect," *ISS Monograph Series* No. 119 (May 2005), available at: http://www.iss.co.za/pubs/Monographs/No119/Mono119.pdf

25. Roberta Cohen and William G.O'Neill, "Last Stand in Sudan?" *Brookings Institution,* March/April 2006, available at: http://www.brookings.edu/research/articles/2006/03/spring-darfur-cohen02

26. For Algeria's key foreign policy principles, see Seghir Rahmani, "Algerian-American Relations (1962–1985): The Study of Algeria's Anti-Imperialist Foreign Policy and its Impact on Algerian-American Relations," PhD dissertation, Georgetown University, 1985.

Undoubtedly, Africa has been important for Algeria in pursuing some of its foreign policy objectives and its roles as liberation supporter, developer and mediator. The next section shows how Algeria used the OAU as a forum from which to disseminate the ideas that would serve its national interests.

The OAU: A Platform for Algeria's Foreign Policy

By the 1970s, the anti-colonial, anti-imperialist ideas and the sovereignty of developing states over their natural resources were promoted at the UN in the struggle for a NIEO.[27] These principles were promoted by President Houari Boumedienne (1965-78) and defended at the UN General Assembly in April 1974. In fact, three years before, at the June 1971 summit in Addis Ababa five months after Algeria nationalised its hydrocarbon resources, the OAU adopted a resolution on the sovereignty of African states over their natural resources, a resolution Boumedienne defended at the UN. This was consistent with the anti-imperialist role Algeria espoused and served as a model for other African states. In its role as supporter of liberation, Algeria was instrumental in OAU decision to admit the Sahrawi Arab Democratic Republic (SADR) as the 51st full member of the organisation in 1982.[28] This decision prompted Morocco to leave the OAU in 1984, when SADR President Mohamed Abdelaziz attended the summit for the first time.[29] Algeria's position on Western Sahara was consistent with its and many African states' support for national liberation movements and the right to self-determination. Algeria also contributed a great deal to Afro-Arab dialogue and to economic and financial cooperation between Africa and the Arab world after the Arab-Israeli war of 1973.[30] It was also influential in enticing the OAU and its member states to show solidarity with Arab states and build a common front against Zionism, apartheid, colonialism and other forms of oppression. The basic plan, initiated by Algeria, was to incorporate Arab-

---

27. Robert A. Mortimer, "Global Economy and African Policy: The Algerian Model," *African Studies Review*, 27, 1 (March 1984):1–22. See, also Robert Malley. *The Call from Algeria: Third Worldism, Revolution, and the Turn to Islam* (Berkeley and Los Angeles: University of California Press, 1996).

28. For a recent work on the reasons Algeria supports the Sahrawis, see Jacob Mundy, "Algeria and the Western Sahara Dispute," *The Maghreb Center Journal*, 1 (Spring/Summer 2010), available at: http://maghrebcenter.files.wordpress.com/2011/07/maghrebcenter-journal-mundy_algeria-w-sahara.pdf

29. P. Mweti Munya, "The Organization of African Unity and its Role in Regional Conflict Resolution and Dispute Settlement: A Critical Evaluation," *Boston College Third World Law Journal*, 19, 2 (1999):561–65; Azzedine Layachi, *The OAU and Western Sahara: A Case Study. The OAU after Thirty Years,* in Yassin El-Ayouty (ed.), (Westport, CT. Praeger, 1994), pp. 27–41.

30. Chikh, *L'Algérie porte de l'Afrique*, pp. 216 ff.

African dialogue into an independent global strategy for countries to control their natural resources.[31]

Undoubtedly, Algeria significantly shaped many of the OAU's decisions in the economic and political realms. Algeria deployed some of its best diplomats to strengthen the OAU and establish solid bilateral relations with African states and liberation movements. Algeria's activism within the OAU to promote its ideas and to garner support from member states proved relatively successful.

However, that activism abated due to the great turmoil that destabilised Algeria in the 1990s: the country was in virtual international isolation due to internal civil conflict that pitted security forces against Islamist insurgents. Besides, the regime had lost its former prestige, especially in the West,[32] and was practically struggling for survival. Even so, Algeria regularly participated in OAU summits and most African countries supported Algeria in OAU forums and avoided criticism of Algerian authorities in the war against the Islamist insurgents.[33] As will be shown below, although Algeria sought closer rapprochement with the US and EU, Africa remained high on its foreign policy agenda. Indeed, one can argue that Algeria's new role as regional and international anti-terrorist actor was first unveiled in the OAU.

Revival Passes through Africa

In July 1999, by which time relative security had returned to the country,[34] and less than three months after Abdelaziz Bouteflika assumed the presidency, Algeria hosted the 35th OAU summit, which was impressively attended.[35] The hosting of the summit was the prelude to a diplomatic offensive to reassert Algeria's leading role in Africa, but also to counter Egyptian, Libyan and Moroccan aspirations. In the 1990s, Morocco, for instance, succeeded in persuading many African countries to withdraw their support from the SADR, support that Algeria had assisted in securing. Libya, for its part, sought an influential presence in Africa through the Community of Sahel-Saharan States (CEN-SAD), established in February 1998 and not including Algeria, and

---

31. Ibid., p. 217.
32. Yahia H. Zoubir, "The Algerian Crisis in World Affairs," *Journal of North African Studies*, 4, 3 (Fall 1999):15–28.
33. Arabic News, 30 January 1998. "Arab Parliamentary delegation in Algeria for Solidarity," http://www.arabicnews.com/ansub/Daily/Day/981030/1998010313.html
34. Yahia H. Zoubir, "Security and the Prospects of Democratisation in Algeria," *Jane's Defence Weekly*, 9 August 1999, p. 19. The security forces had scored substantial successes against the insurgents, an important part of whom (the Islamic Salvation Army) had surrendered in September 1997 in exchange for amnesty.
35. Forty-five (38 heads of state, one vice-president,and six prime-ministers) of the 53 OAU member states attended.

through generous financing of many states. Furthermore, Algeria was intent on reviving its involvement in the resolution of other African conflicts (for example Ethiopia and Eritrea, the Great Lakes), thus reasserting its former role as mediator (including between Iran and the US). The Algiers summit was widely regarded as successful by participants, but especially for Algerians, who saw it as the first step in legitimising the country's return to the international stage and an opportunity to regain influence in world affairs.[36] Guaranteeing the security of all participants was in itself proof of the solidity of the regime. The summit was also an opportunity for Bouteflika to gain legitimacy domestically.[37] At the meeting, Algerians secured the adoption of the OAU Convention on the Prevention and Combating of Terrorism, which was signed by the vast majority of African countries in attendance. Given Algeria's recent history, the country sought the creation of institutions within the organisation that would counter the threat of terrorism more effectively. The OAU's position on terrorism reflected Algeria's own stance throughout the 1990s: terrorism was a transnational phenomenon; a violation of human rights and fundamental freedoms; and represented a serious threat to the stability and security of states and their national institutions as well as to international peace and security.[38] Algeria sought to use the OAU as a platform that would enable it to express its position in a much larger setting, namely, the UN:

> [W]e call for ... effective and efficient international cooperation which should be given concrete expression, under the auspices of OAU, through a speedy conclusion of a Global International Convention for the Prevention and Control of Terrorism in all its forms and the convening of an International Summit Conference under the auspices of the UN to consider this phenomenon and the means to combat it. Africa wants to make its full contribution by adopting its own Convention on this matter.[39]

The adoption of the OAU convention on terrorism was one of Algeria's great successes, since it reinforced the country's leadership role in the war against terrorism. Its other summit success was the nudging of African states to reject forceful seizures of power – unconstitutional changes of government – and

---

36. Zoubir, "The Resurgence of Algeria's Foreign Policy in the Twenty-First Century."
37. Six contenders withdrew on the eve of the election because they believed the military had skewed the process in favour of Bouteflika .
38. Declarations and Decisions Adopted by the Thirty-Fifth Assembly of Heads of State and Government Assembly of Heads of State and Government-Thirty-Fifth Ordinary Session of OAU/Third Ordinary Session of AEC 12-14 July 1999 AHG/Decl. 1–2 (XXXV)-Algiers, Algeria AHG/Dec. 132-142 (XXXV)AHG/OAU/AEC/Dec.1 (III).
39. Ibid.

accept the threat of exclusion of authors of coups from the organisation.[40] This was seen as "a landmark decision,"[41] and has since become an important component of the AU Charter. As will be seen, although Algerian authorities pushed for the adoption of this principle, they bluntly transgressed it in 2008 when they amended the constitution to extend the presidential term limit to allow Boutef-lika to secure a third mandate.

In the next section, we will see how Algeria endeavoured to extend its influence to other areas, such as global economic relations and issues of governance.

Algeria's New Role in the AU: Economy, Governance and Terrorism

While fighting terrorism in the 1990s, Algeria recognised its dependency on Northern countries and understood the need to adopt a more pragmatic, flexible foreign policy. The country had abandoned its radical international policies and had also introduced neoliberal domestic economic reforms and sought integration into the global economy. Obviously, these new orientations overlapped with the new approach in Africa, for, since its inception in 2002, the AU has shifted focus from supporting liberation movements in African territories formerly under colonialism and apartheid, as envisaged by the OAU and the AU's Constitutive Act, and conflict management, to spearheading Africa's development and integration as well as greater cooperation with the North.

Algeria was one of the five founders of the July 2001 New African Initiative, which in October became the NEPAD initiative.[42] NEPAD's primary objectives are poverty eradication, sustainable development and integrating Africa into the global economy. These objectives are far from those ideas Algeria pursued in the 1970s for the creation of a NIEO. NEPAD, which came under AU purview in 2002 and was adopted at the March 2007 Algiers summit as the

---

40. AHG/Dec. 142 (XXXV) the Assembly of Heads of State and Government, decided that "Member States whose Governments came to power through unconstitutional means after the Harare Summit, should restore constitutional legality before the next summit." Assembly of Heads of State and Government Thirty-fifth Ordinary Session of OAU/Third Ordinary Session of AEC 12–14 July 1999. AHG/Decl. 1–2 (XXXV) Algiers, Algeria AHG/Dec. 132–142 (XXXV) AHG/OAU/AEC/Dec.1 (III) Declarations and Decisions Adopted by the Thirty Fifth Assembly of Heads of State and Government. This posture on illegal seizure of power or unconstitutional change of government became an important component of the Lomé "Declaration on the Framework for an OAU Response to Unconstitutional Changes of Government," July 2000 (OAU 2000), the Constitutive Act of the AU (2002), and of the African Charter on Democracy, Elections and Governance, adopted in Addis Ababa in January 2007. See Issaka K. Souaré, "African Union as a norm entrepreneur on military coups d'état in Africa (1952–2012): An empirical assessment," unpublished manuscript (January 2013). I would like to thank Dr. Souaré for sharing his paper with me before publication.
41. Interview with Salim Ahmed Salim, Dar es Salaam, 5 September 2012.
42. African Union, NEPAD Planning and Coordinating Agency, http://www.nepad.org/history

AU's instrument of development, advocates Africa's integration into the global neoliberal order,[43] thus reflecting the Washington Consensus. Algerians have now, like their NEPAD peers, set a development course based on cooperation with developed countries, with Africans purportedly taking a leadership role in the process.

Unconstitutional government change is another issue Algerians were instrumental in getting addressed by other heads of state and of government. At the OAU summit in Algiers, Algerians pushed for a resolution forbidding the unconstitutional seizure of power (Res. 142). This was subsequently adopted at the 2000 OAU summit in Lomé, Togo. Algerian officials argue that economic and social development cannot occur without good governance, including transparency at all levels, an approach meant to depict Bouteflika as a genuine democrat. Thus, they were among the strongest supporters of the 2002 Durban Declaration on Democracy, Political, Economic and Corporate Governance: Algeria not only supported the African Peer Review Mechanism (APRM), but was among the first African countries to volunteer for evaluation by peers (2003). The first report was submitted in 2007 and the second in 2012.[44] This decision has had a spill-over effect, and more AU members are subjecting themselves voluntarily to this process.

Yet in 2006, Algeria, along with Nigeria, succeeded in defeating a definition that would have made it impossible to amend a constitution[45] so as to change presidential term limits,[46] because Bouteflika was already seeking a third term.[47] Only an amendment to the constitution would allow him to do so. The lifting

43. For a criticism of NEPAD from the left, see Patrick Bond, "African development /governance, South African sub-imperialism and NEPAD," paper Presented to IDEAs, Ethiopian Economic Association and the Council for the Development of Social Science Research in Africa Conference on Agrarian Constraint and Poverty Reduction, Addis Ababa, 17-19 December 2004, http://www.networkideas.org/feathm/dec2004/ft03_Ethiopia_Conference_Index.htm

44. See Yahia H. Zoubir, "Governance in Algeria: The Protracted Transition to Democratic Rule," in Abbas Kadhim (ed.), *Governance in the Middle East and North Africa: A Handbook* (London and New York: Routledge, 2013), pp. 451–63.

45. The article which the author obtained in confidence from a member of the judicial commission, stated that it considered unconstitutional, "Une modification ou un détournement d'un texte fondamental ou constitutionnel applicables, à des fins politiques ou électorales, attentatoires au principe de l'alternance politique." In other words, one cannot change or manipulate articles of the constitution in order to be reelected.

46. Issaka K. Souaré, "Presidential Term Limits as an Issue of Peace and Security in Africa," AU Peace and Security Department, Discussion paper for CEWS and desk officers, 10 August 2012, p.6. I would like to thank the author for sharing this paper with me.

47. Ahmed Aghrout and Yahia Zoubir, "Introducing Algeria's President-for-Life," *Middle East Report Online*, April 1, 2009, available at: http://www.merip.org/mero/mero040109, accessed 13 January 2012.

of that obstacle enabled him to run for and win a third term in April 2009.[48] It can be argued that this infringed Article 23 (5) of the African Charter on Democracy, Elections and Governance, which stipulates that "any amendment or revision of the constitution or legal instruments, which is an infringement on the principles of democratic change of government … constitute[s] an unconstitutional change of government and shall draw appropriate sanctions by the Union."[49] Incidentally, Algeria did not sign the Charter until 14 July 2012 and has yet to ratify it.

Besides pursuing an economic and "good" governance agenda, an African antiterrorism agenda is another area, perhaps the most important, where Algeria has had a strong influence on AU policy-making. Throughout the 1990s, Algerians tried to attract world attention to their view that terrorism is a global phenomenon.[50] Algerian policy-makers felt partly vindicated after 9/11, when both the US and Europe came to espouse a similar position on terrorism.[51] Predictably, Algeria joined the war on terrorism that the US administration launched on the morrow of those attacks.[52] As noted earlier, Algerian authorities had elevated the fight against terrorism to the multilateral level during the 35 OAU summit in Algiers. At Algeria's initiative, the 1999 OAU Convention on the Prevention and Combating of Terrorism was followed by an action plan adopted at the intergovernmental high level meeting of AU member states, held in Algiers in September 2002. Unsurprisingly, Algeria had already played a key role in the promulgation of the Protocol Relating to the Establishment of the Peace and Security Council of the African Union adopted by the AU inaugural summit in Durban in July 2002. Algerians made clear their willingness to take the lead in the fight terrorism in Africa. For example, on 5 July 2002, Minister for Maghreb and African Affairs Abdelkader Messahel declared that, "Algeria, which has constantly called for international cooperation to prevent this bane [of terrorism] … is prepared to make its experience in the prevention and fight

---

48. Yahia H. Zoubir and Ahmed Aghrout, "Algeria's Path to Reform: Authentic Change?" *Middle East Policy*, 19, 2 (2012):66–83.

49. African Union, *African Charter on Democracy,* Elections and Governance, 30 January 2007, available at: http://www.au.int/en/content/african-charter-democracy-elections-and-governance

50. See "Allocution du président Bouteflika prononcée à l'ouverture du colloque international sur le terrorisme," APS, 26 October 2002, reprinted in *Algeria Watch*, available at : http://www.algeria-watch.org/farticle/colloque_terrorisme/allocution_bouteflika.htm

51. Most Algerian officials the author interviewed aver that events proved them right and that the West should have listened to them earlier. They also insist they had been abandoned to face terrorism alone. These arguments are repeated in the press.

52. Yahia H. Zoubir, "Algeria and U.S. Interests: Containing Radical Islamism and Promoting Democracy," *Middle East Policy*, 9, 1 (March 2002):64–81.

against this bane ... available to the international community, particularly to the member states of our organization [African Union]."[53]

Algerian officials view the war against terrorism in a broad sense: it includes the need for addressing by many means the peaceful resolution of conflicts, good governance and democracy as a *sine qua non* for socioeconomic development, all of them implicit in the NEPAD concept. Thus, one of the main missions of the Peace and Security Council (PSC), modelled on the UN Security Council, is the promotion of peace, security and stability in Africa, and also coordinating and harmonising "continental efforts in the prevention and combating of international terrorism in all its aspects," in short, the implementation of the OAU Convention on the Prevention and Combating of Terrorism.[54] Algerians saw the PSC as a vehicle for the AU to address a variety of security and terrorism issues on the continent. In 2004, Bouteflika declared that the PSC's role in this regard "is decisive" and welcomed the protocol added to the Algiers Convention on Terrorism.[55] In the same speech, Bouteflika announced the creation of the African Centre for Studies and Research on Terrorism (ACSRT) in Algiers.[56] The ACSRT was designed by Saïd Djinnit, a seasoned Algerian diplomat who was the first commissioner of the AU's Peace and Security department (July 2003 to April 2008).[57] The centre produces reports on terrorism that the PSC uses for its own analyses and assists in the implementation of international conventions relating to terrorism.[58] It also serves as a monitoring and alerting tool for the AU and its members by incorporating the concept of preventive crisis management. The non-appointment of an Algerian to head the ACSRT rests on an AU tradition not to assign a local as head of an African organisation, even if the deputy may be a local, as has hitherto been the case with the ACSRT. Perhaps the biggest success of Algerian diplomacy since the close of the 1990s was

53. MAE (Ministry of Foreign Affairs), Algiers, 9 July 2002, http://www.mae.dz/ma_fr/stories.php?story=05/02/08/6234208

54. http://www.au.int/en/content/protocol-oau-convention-prevention-and-combating-terrorism

55. MAE, 6 July 2004, "Texte intégral du discours du président de la République, M. Abdelaziz Bouteflika, prononcé mercredi devant la 3ème Conférence des chefs d'Etat et de Gouvernement de l'Union Africaine qui se tient depuis mardi à Addis Abeba," http://www.mae.dz/ma_fr/stories.php?story=04/07/07/7231159

56. http://www.caert.org.dz/. The decision to create ACSRT was made at the Inter-Governmental High Level Meeting on the Prevention and Combating of Terrorism in Africa, Algiers, 11–14 September 2002. The meeting adopted the related plan of action. The initiative was inspired by Algeria.

57. Author's interviews with Saïd Djinnit, Dakar, Senegal, 23 March 2011; Addis Ababa, 29 January 2013. Djinnit also contributed to the development of the AU's Peace and Security Architecture, the Agenda of the PSC and the African Standby Force. He is currently the UN Special Representative to West Africa.

58. See, "Modalities for the functioning of the African Center for Studies and Research on Terrorism (ACSRT)," available at: http://www.caert.org.dz/an/mandat.php

convincing African leaders of the linkages between terrorism and other plagues, such as the proliferation of weapons of mass destruction, illicit proliferation of small arms and light weapons, money laundering and drug trafficking.[59] Successive Algerian ambassadors to Ethiopia and the OAU/AU, as well as military attachés and ambassadors to African countries, worked determinedly to persuade their counterparts of the correctness of Algeria's analysis and policy on terrorism. African leaders whose countries experienced terrorism could only concur with the Algerian position.

The election of Algerian diplomats to high-level positions reflects the credibility that Algeria enjoys within the AU. This is particularly apparent in the PSC: the two successive Commissioners for Peace and Security, Saïd Djinnit and Ramtane Lamamra, are among the most experienced Algerian diplomats.[60] However, Algerian officials insist that Algeria, which contributes 15 per cent of the AU budget, is careful not to make hegemonic claims: "Algeria can sway the AU in its direction without, however, putting great pressure."[61] It is perhaps true that Algerians feel they are among the natural leaders of the continent because of the legitimacy earned through one of the bloodiest wars of national liberation, but this feeling also derives from the rejection of any colonialist, racist mentality towards Africans in general.

Algerians instead seek to persuade their African colleagues with rational arguments conveyed by experienced diplomats who can help to promote the continent's well-being. For instance, Algeria obtained support on the criminalisation of ransom-payments to hostage takers without "undue" pressure on African leaders. Indeed, Algeria has fought hard for this criminalisation: Algerians have argued forcefully that in addition to the funds terrorists obtained from their association with drug-traffickers (a subject the Algerians have warned the international community about for many years[62]), they finance their activities through ransoms received from some states. Thus, in 2009, Algeria succeeded in having the AU pass a resolution on this matter. The resolution "strongly condemns the payment of ransoms to terrorist groups for hostages to be freed."[63] The AU, with "strong nudging" from Algeria, endorsed the principle that, "ter-

---

59. Interview with senior Algerian official, Ministry of Foreign Affairs, Algiers, 4 September 2011.
60. In 2008, Ambassador Ramtane Lamamra was elected with 31 votes. In July 2012, he was reelected overwhelmingly (42 votes). Algeria was elected to the PSC in 2004, 2007, and in 2013. In 2013, Algeria was elected with 34 votes, more than the 2/3rd votes required for such election. In 2010, Libya was elected as the representative for North Africa in the PSC.
61. Interview with senior Algerian official, 2 September 2012 (place not mentioned at official's request).
62. Interview with senior ranking officer, Ministry of Defence, Algiers, 3 September 2011.
63. African Union, "Decisions and Declarations – Assembly of the African Union Thirteenth Ordinary Session 1–3 July 2009 Sirte," Great Socialist People's Libyan Arab Jamahiriya Assembly/AU/Dec. 243-267 (XIII) Rev.1 Assembly/AU/Decl.1–5(XIII).

rorism is a threat to human rights" and "cannot be justified under any circum-stances," and that the AU Council is determined to combat this scourge in all its forms. In fact, Algeria has been trying to get the UN to adopt a similar resolu-tion on ransoms, the AU having served as a necessary step along the way. Even though Algerians have not obtained such a clear UN resolution, they can find consolation in UN Security Council Resolution 1904 of 2009, which contains provisions criminalising such payments.[64]

Since the 1990s, then, Algeria's foreign policy shifted from liberation sup-porter to leading in the war against terrorism. This role is evident in the Afri-can Union, which Algeria has succeeded in convincing to focus on peace and security and to create new structures to address terrorism and conflicts. As shall be seen in the next sections, Algeria and the AU have identical positions on the crisis in the Sahel in general and in Mali in particular.

The African Union, Algeria, and the Crisis in the Sahel

A major concern of the AU in early 2012 was the instability in northern Mali, aggravated by the return of Tuareg fighters from Libya.[65] The AU strongly con-demned these events, which "highlight the importance and urgency of enhanc-ing regional cooperation and coordination among the concerned Member States to more effectively address the security challenges in the Sahelo-Saharan belt."[66] The Union reiterated its commitment to the unity, territorial integrity and sov-ereignty of Mali and rejected the recourse to armed rebellion. This was echoed by the Panel of the Wise, which had been presided over by Algeria's Ahmed Ben Bella until his death a month prior to its meeting in Tunis in April 2012. The panel expressed its "deep concern about the situation in northern Mali. It stressed the need for a collective and determined African action, with the support of the international community, to preserve the unity and territorial integrity of Mali. The Panel condemned the action of the armed and terrorist groups operating in northern Mali."[67] The coup in Bamako on 22 March 2012, which violated the AU Charter principle against unconstitutional changes of

---

64. Security Council, SC/9825. *Security Council Amends United Nations Al-Qaida/Taliban Sanctions Regime, Authorizes Appointment of Ombudsperson to Handle Delisting Issues,* 17 December 2009, available at: http://www.un.org/News/Press/docs/2009/sc9825.doc.htm

65. See, Yahia H. Zoubir, "Qaddafi's Spawn: What the Dictator's Demise Unleashed in the Middle East " *Foreign Affairs,* 24 July 2012, available at: http://www.foreignaffairs.com/articles/137796/yahia-h-zoubir/qaddafis-spawn

66. African Union, "Press Release: The African Union Condemns the Attacks Perpetrated by Armed Groups in the Northern Part of Mali and Affirms its Full Support to the Malian Government," Addis Ababa, 18 January 2012, available at: http://www.peaceau.org/up-loads/com-.auc.mali.18.01-en.pdf

67. African Union, 12th Meeting of the Panel of the Wise of the African Union, Tunis, Repub-lic of Tunisia, 30 April 2012, Pow/Pr/Comm (XII), available at: http://www.peaceau.org/uploads/panel-of-the-wise-tunisia-30-04-12-2-.pdf

government, had exacerbated an already complex situation in the country and region in general.

It is within this context that Algeria articulated its position. As shall be seen in the next sub-section, Algeria's policy towards conflict in the Sahel/Mali chimes with the views of the AU.

Algeria and the Crisis in the Sahel

The crisis in the Sahel, particularly Mali, presented Algeria with a challenge not seen since the war in Western Sahara in the 1970s and the internal strife of the 1990s. The situation in Mali, which shares 1,400 kilometre border with Algeria that is difficult to control, has raised serious concerns about Algeria's national security.

A number of factors account for the attention paid this region by Algeria, but also by its neighbours and extra-regional powers. First, there are the natural resources for which traditional and emerging powers (China, the EU, US, India, Russia and Brazil) compete. Second, there is the presence of jihadists, mainly Al-Qaida in the Islamic Maghreb (AQIM), which Algerian security forces pushed southward beyond the country's borders, and the Movement for Oneness and Jihad in West Africa (MUJAO), and the concomitant failure of fragile Sahelian states to impose authority over their territories.[68] Third, there is the potential of the area to become a new haven for terrorists, the so-called "Sahelistan", where terrorists, including the Nigerian Boko Haram, can train and prepare operations against regional and international governments: the attack on the In Amenas gas plant in southern Algeria on 16 January 2013 illustrates this point. Lastly, there is the question of the Tuareg, who form minorities in Algeria, Burkina Faso, Chad, Libya Mali, and Niger. For Algeria, which boasts a Tuareg minority in the south, this is a salient issue and explains Algeria's approach to separate the terrorists from the Tuareg and other minorities in northern Mali.[69]

The government has enrolled other core countries of the region (Mali, Mauritania, Niger, and even Nigeria) in a concerted regional strategy to contain AQIM by cutting off support to the terrorist groups. Furthermore, Algerians have sought the support of the Sahel countries for their vision of settling regional security problems without the involvement of foreign powers, except in sectoral cooperation. Clearly, the Sahel is of paramount importance to Algeria's national security.

---

68. See Lothar Brock, Hans-Henrik Holm, Georg Sørensen, and Michael Stohl, *Fragile State: Violence and the Failure of Intervention* (Cambridge: Polity, 2012); Charles T. Call, "Beyond the 'Failed State': Toward Conceptual Alternatives," *European Journal of International Relations,* XX, 10 (April 2010):1–24.
69. Yahia H. Zoubir, "Algeria and the Sahelian Imbroglio: Preventing War and Fighting Terrorism," Aljazeera Center for Studies, 25 November 2012, available at: http://studies.aljazeera.net/ResourceGallery/media/Documents/2012/11/25/20121125957287205 80Algeria%20and%20the%20Sahelian%20Imbroglio.pdf

Regional Cooperation Initiatives

Algeria has played a leading role in the creation of regional organisations, such as the Common Operational Joint-Chiefs of Staff Committee (CEMOC), located in Tamanrasset, and the Unified Fusion and Liaison (UFL), the intelligence arm of the core countries, located in the ACSRT compound. This ambitious strategy faced major hurdles, not least the strong relations Mali, Mauritania and Niger have with France, which partly explain the suspicions among the core countries. The presence of terrorist groups and drug traffickers in the Sahara-Sahel strengthened Algeria's arguments regarding the need to fight terrorism through multilateral cooperation, while avoiding foreign intervention, a perspective prevalent in the AU. Algeria has sought a leadership role in the battle against terrorism because it is the richest country and has the most powerful military in the region. Algerians have developed a strategy they were able to expound with relative success within the AU and have helped Mali in various ways (supply of weapons, financial assistance, etc.). They have also organised conferences to generate shared views on terrorism and how to counter it regionally and internationally.[70] The PSC has also called for international cooperation, to which Algeria has responded with concrete measures.[71]

The AU and Algeria: Resolving the Crisis in Mali

Until France's military intervention on 11 January 2013, Algeria pursued a two-track policy.[72] Firstly, it tried to disconnect the Tuareg and other segments of the population in northern Mali from the terrorist groups. It also urged the government in Bamako to initiate dialogue with the Islamist Tuareg of Ansar el Dine (which for a time opposed partition of Mali, but sought to impose Shari'a law in its northern parts). Secondly, Algeria urged Bamako to engage in dialogue with the secularist MNLA, whose leaders had proclaimed the independence

---

70. See, for instance, African Union, "Press Release: Opening In Algiers of an Experts' Meeting on the Draft African Model Law on Counter-Terrorism.The meeting also witnessed the inauguration of the African Union Special Representative for Counter-Terrorism Cooperation," Addis Ababa, 15 December 2010.

71. Algeria responded by organising an international conference on the Sahel entitled, "Partnership, Security, and Development," on 7–8 September 2010. It involved the "core countries" and various external actors, The conference served as a forum for Algeria to disseminate the principles inscribed in the AU foundational documentsSee the detailed conference report by Ghania Oukazi, "L'Algérie appelle la communauté internationale à respecter la résolution onusienne criminalisant le paiement des rançons et à élaborer une stratégie commune pour lutter contre le terrorisme et le crime transnational organisé." *Le Quotidien d'Oran*, 8 September 2011, http://www.lequotidien-oran.com/index.php?news=5157499&archive_date=2011-09-08

72. Interview with Abdelkader Messahel, Algerian minister delegate for African and Maghreb affairs, Addis Ababa, 25 January 2013. See also, MAE, "Crise malienne: 'l'intégrité territoriale du Mali n'est pas négociable (M. MESSAHEL)," 24 June 2012, http://www.mae.dz/ma_fr/stories.php?story=12/06/25/7230634

of Azawad on 6 April 2012.[73] This policy was consistent with the AU's call for dialogue. Both Algeria and the AU condemned the coup in Mali, which exacerbated the crisis, and favoured the MNLA's defeat of Malian troops in the north. Algerians believed that a negotiated political solution to the conflict in northern Mali could be found through dialogue with groups opposed to terrorism. While Algerian policy-makers empathise with Malian Tuareg, they are suspicious of Tuareg claims to autonomy or irredentism. They also reacted negatively to the MNLA's proclamation of an independent state, in keeping with Algeria's and AU policy, which opposes secessionist movements and rejects claims by political, social or ethnic categories that could jeopardise the internationally recognised national unity and territorial integrity of a state. Secessionist tendencies are seen as a threat to Algeria's own national security and territorial integrity. This is the reason Algeria has repeatedly played a key role in mediating between the Tuareg of northern Mali and the government in Bamako – in the 1990s, in 2006 and again in 2012.[74] However, it is wrong to assume that Algeria was opposed to military intervention in Mali or is soft on terrorism.[75] Quite the contrary. State officials declared publicly that it was "legitimate" to use all means, "including force" to eradicate terrorist groups and their transnational organised crime affiliates in the Sahel.[76] However, for Algeria's policy-makers, military intervention should be the last resort. The prime minister commented: "We believe … the use of force must be conducted with the necessary discernment to avoid amalgamation and confusion between the peoples of northern Mali, who have legitimate claims, and terrorist groups and drug traffickers, who … are the source of the threats in the region."[77] This was consistent with the position of the AU, which urged the Malian transitional authorities to establish "the … national structure that will … [conduct] negotiations with Malian armed groups … willing to engage in dialogue to find a political solution … on the basis of … strict respect for the national unity and territorial integrity of Mali, rejection of terrorism and transnational organised crime, as well as armed rebellion."[78] Although Algeria was opposed to foreign intervention in the Sahel,

---

73. Yahia H. Zoubir, "The Sahara-Sahel Quagmire: Regional and International Ramifications," *Mediterranean Politics*, 17, 3 (2012):452–58.

74. For more details, see, Zoubir, "Algeria and the Sahelian Imbroglio.".

75. Interviews with African officials, September and November 2012.

76. AE, "M. SELLAL: l'Algérie en faveur du dialogue pour une solution politique à la crise malienne," 18 December 2012, http://www.mae.dz/ma_fr/stories.php?story=12/12/19/0584440

77. MAE, "Sahel: l'éradication du terrorisme et du crime organisé par tous les moyens, y compris par le recours à la force, 11 October 2012, " http://www.mae.dz/ma_fr/stories.php?story=12/10/11/3005099

78. African Union, "Conclusions: Meeting of the Support and Follow-Up Group on The Situation in Mali," Bamako, 19 October 2012, http://www.safpi.org/news/article/2012/au-peace-and-security-council-communique-mali.

it assisted France by allowing the use of Algeria's airspace, when the troops of Ansar Edine joined AQIM and the MUJAO in an attempt to conquer the south of Mali. The reaction of the AU was no different from Algeria's: it condemned unequivocally the military coup in Mali,[79] as well as the MNLA's proclamation of independence, recalling "the fundamental principle of the intangibility of borders inherited by the African countries at their accession to independence and reiterate[ing] AU's unwavering commitment to the national unity and territorial integrity of the Republic of Mali."[80]

Algerian policy-makers are convinced that Algeria's position has also been shared by the international community in general.[81] There is consensus among them that the territorial integrity and sovereignty of Mali are non-negotiable and that the legitimate claims of the Tuareg and other minorities in northern Mali should be resolved within Mali's institutional framework.

The necessity of dialogue with the populations of northern Mali has not subsided, because a military victory over the terrorist groups does not address the deep causes of the instability in northern Mali. However, the Malian government, feeling empowered by French and ECOWAS support, seems divided on the need for dialogue with non-terrorist Tuareg and the Arabs in the north,[82] in spite of international support for this, including by the US[83] and even France.[84]

The situation in northern Mali illustrates the similarity of views between

---

79. African Union, "The African Union Strongly Condemns the Action of the Mutineers Who Announced that They Have Taken Power in Mali," *Press Release*, Addis Ababa, 22 March 2012, http://www.au.int/en/dp/cpauc_former/content/african-union-strongly-condemns-action-mutineers-who-announced-they-have-taken-power-mali

80. African Union, "The African Union Totally Rejects the so-called Declaration of 'Independence' by a Rebel Group In Northern Mali," *Press Release,* Addis Ababa, 6 April 2012, http://ps.au.int/en/content/african-union-strongly-condemns-abduction-consul-and-diplomats-algerias-consulate-gao-mali-1

81. Interview with Abdelkader Messahel, Algerian minister delegate for African and Maghreb affairs, Addis Ababa, 25 January 2013.

82. Kharroubi Habib, "Crise malienne: Bamako sans enthousiasme pour la feuille de route politique," *Afrique-Asie,* 7 February 2013, available at: http://www.afrique-asie.fr/menu/afrique/4904-crise-malienne-bamako-sans-enthousiasme-pour-la-feuille-de-route-politique.html

83. See, Statement by Secretary of State John Kerry, as well as UN Secretary General Ban ki-Moon on 14 February 2013, http://www.dailymotion.com/video/xxijrc_kerry-and-un-chief-to-discuss-future-of-mali_news

84. French Ministry of Foreign Affairs, France Diplomatie, "Mali - Feuille de route pour la transition (28 janvier2013)," available at: http://www.diplomatie.gouv.fr/fr/pays-zones-geo/mali/la-france-et-le-mali/evenements-19439/article/mali-feuille-de-route-pour-la; The European Union Council also urged the Malian government to initiate talks with the armed non-terrorist groups. See, "Conseil de l'Union Européenne, Conclusions du Conseil relatives au Mali," *3222ème session du Conseil AFFAIRES ETRANGERES, Bruxelles, 18 février 2013,* available at: http://www.consilium.europa.eu/uedocs/cms_data/docs/pressdata/FR/foraff/135523.pdf. The Malian government set up a Commission for Dialogue on 6 March 2013.

Algeria and the AU: the AU's position is in large part due to Algeria's skilful diplomacy within AU structures. This was also evident during the first six months of the Libyan rebellion in 2011. Algeria and the AU concurred that, ultimately, only a political solution would make it possible to meet, in a sustainable way, the legitimate aspirations of the Libyan people for reform, democracy, good governance and the rule of law.[85] In short, self-determination remains the premise for Algeria's and the AU's efforts and the core of their "convictions." Both interpreted UN Resolution 1973 as limited to the protection of civilians and not as endorsing NATO's and Western interference in Libya's domestic affairs or regime change.

In sum, the AU's and Algeria's positions on the Mali crisis were practically identical: both rejected the unconstitutional change of government (as decided in Algiers in 1999), as well as the MNLA's secessionist attempt, based on a shared commitment to "defend the sovereignty, territorial integrity and independence of its Member States."

Conclusion

Algeria has been one of the staunchest supporters of the OAU and AU. It has been involved in the creation of virtually all the structures of the two organisations and has assigned many resources to assist in their evolution. Both OAU and AU have served as platforms for Algeria's to swing these organisations, albeit tactfully, in a direction that reflects Algeria's conception of its national role and choices. Through both bodies, Algeria has been able to exert its influence and counter the policies of its regional rivals within the OAU/AU and their structures (Egypt and Qaddafi's Libya) and without (Morocco). Since the late 1990s, the OAU/AU has allowed Algeria to play its role as anti-terrorist leader, a role that has helped the country regain its lost standing in world affairs and to secure support from the major powers. The country has so far dodged the Arab uprisings, and Algerian policy-makers know that in case of upheaval, the main support they will receive will certainly be from their AU peers, many of whose members have remained loyal to Algeria. Whether such support will persist is open to question, as changes in the Arab world continue to unfold and affect inter-African relations.

The Arab revolts since 2010 have broadened the definition of what constitutes unconstitutional changes of government. Overthrowing the dictatorial regime in Tunisia by peaceful means can hardly be considered as such. But what about Libya, where a peaceful movement turned violent and was then armed by

---

85. See, Jean Ping, "African Union Role in the Libyan Crisis," *Pambazuka*, Issue 563, 15 December 2011, available at: http://pambazuka.org/en/category/aumonitor/78691

outside forces? This is certainly a question the AU continues to grapple with.[86] And, what if Bouteflika decides to run for a fourth term despite his poor health, a circumstance that has contributed to Algeria's current diplomatic paralysis? Regardless of the answer, Algeria will continue to support the AU and use it to defend its national interests and in articulating the ideas that support the roles that Algerian policy-makers espouse at given periods. For now, Algeria is playing its role as anti-terrorist leader. Should Algeria become a prosperous democracy, it is likely that it will play the role of democratic model to further its national interests.

---

86. For an excellent discussion, see, Mehari Taddele Maru, "The North African Uprisings Under the African Union's Normative Framework," Conference on the Implications of North African Uprisings for Sub Saharan Africa, Inter-Africa Group, August 2012, Universal Printing Press, Addis Ababa, http://danielberhane.com/2012/09/30/research-the-north-african-uprisings-and-the-african-union/

About the authors

Mehari Taddele Maru is an international consultant on international law, AU affairs, African peace and security matters and migration and displacement issues. Until August 2012, he was the programme manager for African Conflict Prevention and Risk Analysis at Institute for Security Studies. A former fellow at Harvard and Oxford Universities, he holds a Doctorate of Legal Sciences (DSL) from JL Giessen University, Germany, MPA from Harvard, MSc from Oxford and LLB from Addis Ababa University. Dr Mehari has served as the programme coordinator for migration and as a legal expert at the African Union Commission. He has also worked as director of the Addis Ababa University Office for University Reform.

Thomas Kwasi Tieku has a joint appointment to the Munk School of Global Affairs and New College at the University of Toronto. An award-winning teacher and a former director of African studies at the same university, Tieku's current research focuses on international mediation and negotiation, regional security innovations, international organisation and foreign policy analysis. He has consulted for a number of organisations and governments, including the World Bank, African Union and Canada's Department of Foreign Affairs and International Trade. Tieku's academic works have appeared in *International Journal, Democratisation, African Affairs, Africa Today, and Canadian Foreign Policy Journal.* He is the co-editor of *African Journal of Political Science and International Relations*, and the author of *US-Africa Relations in the Age of Obama*.

Yahia H. Zoubir is professor of international studies and international management, and director of research in geopolitics at EUROMED MANAGEMENT, Marseille School of Management. His recent works include *Global Security Watch: The Maghreb* (ABC/Clio, 2013); "The End of the Libyan Dictatorship: The Uncertain Transition," *Third World Quarterly* (July 2012); "Algeria's Path to Political Reforms: Authentic Reforms?" *Middle East Policy* (July 2012); *North Africa: Politics, Region, and the Limits of Transformation* (Routledge, 2008). He serves on the board of numerous international academic journals. Zoubir is also an international consultant for governments and business.

DISCUSSION PAPERS PUBLISHED BY THE INSTITUTE

Recent issues in the series are available electronically for download free of charge
www.nai.uu.se

1988

1. Kenneth Hermele and Bertil Odén, *Sanctions and Dilemmas. Some Implications of Economic Sanctions against South Africa.* 1988. 43 pp. ISBN 91-7106-286-6

1989

2. Elling Njål Tjønneland, *Pax Pretoriana. The Fall of Apartheid and the Politics of Regional Destabilisation.*

1990

3. Hans Gustafsson, Bertil Odén and Andreas Tegen, *South African Minerals. An Analysis of Western Dependence.*

1991

4. Bertil Egerö, *South African Bantustans. From Dumping Grounds to Battlefronts.*

1994

5. Carlos Lopes, *Enough is Enough! For an Alternative Diagnosis of the African Crisis.*

6. Annika Dahlberg, *Contesting Views and Changing Paradigms.*

1996

7. Bertil Odén, *Southern African Futures. Critical Factors for Regional Development in Southern Africa.*

1997

8. Colin Leys and Mahmood Mamdani, *Crisis and Reconstruction – African Perspectives.*

2001

9. Gudrun Dahl, *Responsibility and Partnership in Swedish Aid Discourse.* 2001. 30 pp. ISBN 91-7106-473-7

10. Henning Melber and Christopher Saunders, *Transition in Southern Africa – Comparative Aspects.* 2001. 28 pp. ISBN 91-7106-480-X

11. *Regionalism and Regional Integration in Africa.*

12. Souleymane Bachir Diagne, et al., *Identity and Beyond: Rethinking Africanity.*

13. Georges Nzongola-Ntalaja, et al., *Africa in the New Millennium.* Edited by Raymond Suttner.

2002

14. *Zimbabwe's Presidential Elections 2002.* Edited by Henning Melber.

15. Birgit Brock-Utne, Language, *Education and Democracy in Africa.*

16. Henning Melber et al., *The New Partnership for Africa's development* (NEPAD).

17. Juma Okuku, *Ethnicity, State Power and the Democratisation Process in Uganda.*

18. Yul Derek Davids, et al., *Measuring Democracy and Human Rights in Southern Africa.* Compiled by Henning Melber.

19. Michael Neocosmos, Raymond Suttner and Ian Taylor, *Political Cultures in Democratic South Africa.* Compiled by Henning Melber.

20. Martin Legassick, *Armed Struggle and Democracy. The Case of South Africa.*

2003

21. Reinhart Kössler, Henning Melber and Per Strand, *Development from Below. A Namibian Case Study.*

22. Fred Hendricks, *Fault-Lines in South African Democracy. Continuing Crises of Inequality and Injustice.*

23. Kenneth Good, *Bushmen and Diamonds. (Un) Civil Society in Botswana.*

24. Robert Kappel, Andreas Mehler, Henning Melber and Anders Danielson, *Structural Stability in an African Context.*

2004

25. Patrick Bond, South Africa and Global Apartheid. *Continental and International Policies and Politics.*

26. Bonnie Campbell (ed.), *Regulating Mining in Africa. For whose benefit?*

2005

27. Suzanne Dansereau and Mario Zamponi, Zimbabwe – *The Political Economy of Decline.* Compiled by Henning Melber.

28. Lars Buur and Helene Maria Kyed, *State Recognition of Traditional Authority in Mozambique. The nexus of Community Representation and State Assistance.*

29. Hans Eriksson and Björn Hagströmer, *Chad – Towards Democratisation or Petro-Dictatorship?*

30. Mai Palmberg and Ranka Primorac (eds), *Skinning the Skunk – Facing Zimbabwean Futures.*

2006

31. Michael Brüntrup, Henning Melber and Ian Taylor, Africa, *Regional Cooperation and the World Market – Socio-Economic Strategies in Times of Global Trade Regimes. Compiled by Henning Melber.*

32. Fibian Kavulani Lukalo, *Extended Handshake or Wrestling Match? – Youth and Urban Culture Celebrating Politics in Kenya.*

33. Tekeste Negash, Education in Ethiopia: *From Crisis to the Brink of Collapse.*

34. Fredrik Söderbaum and Ian Taylor (eds) *Micro-Regionalism in West Africa. Evidence from Two Case Studies.*

35. Henning Melber (ed.), *On Africa – Scholars and African Studies.*

2007

36. Amadu Sesay, *Does One Size Fit All? The Sierra Leone Truth and Reconciliation Commission Revisited.*

37. Karolina Hulterström, Amin Y. Kamete and Henning Melber, *Political Opposition in African Countries – The Case of Kenya, Namibia, Zambia and Zimbabwe.*

38. Henning Melber (ed.), *Governance and State Delivery in Southern Africa. Examples from Botswana, Namibia and Zimbabwe.*

39. Cyril Obi (ed.), *Perspectives on Côte d'Ivoire: Between Political Breakdown and Post-Conflict Peace.*

2008

40. Anna Chitando, *Imagining a Peaceful Society. A Vision of Children's Literature in a Post-Conflict Zimbabwe.*

2009

41. Olawale Ismail, *The Dynamics of Post-Conflict Reconstruction and Peace Building in West Africa. Between Change and Stability.*

42. Ron Sandrey and Hannah Edinger, *Examining the South Africa– China Agricultural Relationship.*

43. Xuan Gao, *The Proliferation of Anti-Dumping and Poor Governance in Emerging Economies.*

44. Lawal Mohammed Marafa, *Africa's Business and Development Relationship with China. Seeking Moral and Capital Values of the Last Economic Frontier.*

45. Mwangi wa Githinji, *Is That a Dragon or an Elephant on Your Ladder? The Potential Impact of China and India on Export Led Growth in African Countries.*

46. Jo-Ansie van Wyk, Cadres, *Capitalists, Elites and Coalitions. The ANC, Business and Development in South Africa.*

47. Elias Courson, *Movement for the Emancipation of the Niger Delta (MEND). Political Marginalization, Repression and Petro-Insurgency in the Niger Delta.*

2010

48. Babatunde Ahonsi, *Gender Violence and HIV/AIDS in Post-Conflict West Africa. Issues and Responses.*

49. Usman Tar and Abba *Gana Shettima, Endangered Democracy? The Struggle over Secularism and its Implications for Politics and Democracy in Nigeria.*

50. Garth Andrew Myers, *Seven Themes in African Urban Dynamics.*

51. Abdoumaliq Simone, *The Social Infrastructures of City Life in Contemporary Africa.*

2011

52. Li Anshan, *Chinese Medical Cooperation in Africa. With Special Emphasis on the Medical Teams and Anti-Malaria Campaign.*

53. Folashade Hunsu, Zangbeto: *Navigating the Spaces Between Oral art, Communal Security And Conflict Mediation in Badagry, Nigeria.*

54. Jeremiah O. Arowosegbe, *Reflections on the Challenge of Reconstructing Post-Conflict States in West Africa: Insights from Claude Ake's Political Writings.*

55. Bertil Odén, *The Africa Policies of Nordic Countries and the Erosion of the Nordic Aid Model: A comparative study.*

56. Angela Meyer, *Peace and Security Cooperation in Central Africa: Developments, Challenges and Prospects.*

57. Godwin R. Murunga, *Spontaneous or Premeditated? Post-Election Violence in Kenya.*

58. David Sebudubudu & Patrick Molutsi, *The Elite as a Critical Factor in National Development: The Case of Botswana.*

59. Sabelo J. Ndlovu-Gatsheni, *The Zimbabwean Nation-State Project. A Historical Diagnosis of Identity and Power-Based Conflicts in a Postcolonial State.*

60. Jide Okeke, *Why Humanitarian Aid in Darfur is not a Practice of the 'Responsibility to Protect'.*

62. Osita A. Agbu, *Ethnicity and Democratisation in Africa. Challenges for Politics and Development.*

63. Cheryl Hendricks, *Gender and Security in Africa. An Overview.*

64. Adebayo O. Olukoshi, *Democratic Governance and Accountability in Africa. In Search of a Workable Framework.*

65. Christian Lund, *Land Rights and Citizenship in Africa.*

66. Lars Rudebeck, *Electoral Democratisation in Post-Civil War Guinea-Bissau 1999–2008.*

67. Kidane Mengisteab, *Critical Factors in the Horn of Africa's Raging Conflicts.*

68. Solomon T. Ebobrah, *Reconceptualising Democratic Local Governance in the Niger Delta.*

69. Linda Darkwa, *The Challenge of Sub-regional Security in West Africa. The Case of the 2006 Ecowas Convention on Small Arms and Light Weapons.*

70. J.Shola Omotola, *Unconstitutional Changes of Government in Africa. What Implications for Democratic Consolidation?*

71. Wale Adebanwi, *Globally Oriented Citizenship and International Voluntary Service. Interrogating Nigeria's Technical Aid Corps Scheme.*

2012

72. Göran Holmqvist, *Inequality and Identity. Causes of War?*

73. Ike Okonta, *Biafran Ghosts. The MASSOB Ethnic Militia and Nigeria's Democratisation Process.*

74. Li Anshan, Liu Haifang, Pan Huaqiong, Zeng Aiping and He Wenping, *FOCAC Twelve Years Later. Achievements, Challenges and the Way Forward.*

75. Redie Bereketeab, *Self-Determination and Secessionism in Somaliland and South Sudan. Challenges to Postcolonial State-building.*

2013

76. Mikael Eriksson and Linnéa Gelot (eds), *The African Union in Light of the Arab Revolts. An appraisal of the foreign policy and security objectives of Ethiopia, South Africa and Algeria.*

www.ingramcontent.com/pod-product-compliance
Lightning Source LLC
Chambersburg PA
CBHW080209300326
41934CB00039B/3427